Being Black in
AMERICA

SYSTEMIC RACISM
and the African American Experience

Stephen Currie

ReferencePoint
Press

San Diego, CA

About the Author

Stephen Currie is the author of several dozen books for young people, many of them for ReferencePoint Press. He has also taught at grade levels ranging from kindergarten to college. He lives with his family in New York's Hudson Valley.

Picture Credits:
Cover: Rocketclips, Inc./Shutterstock.com
 6: Rawpixel.com/Shutterstock.com
10: Ssgt. Eddie Siguenza/US Air/Zuma Press/Newscom
12: SlobodanMiljevic/iStock
16: pio3/Shutterstock
21: Associated Press
23: SFIO CRACHO/Shutterstock.com
27: Dean Drobot/Shutterstock
32: fizkes/Shutterstock
34: Everett Collection/Newscom
39: Monkey Business Images/Shutterstock
44: Amy Katz/Zuma Press/Newscom
46: Maury Aaseng
50: Johnny Silvercloud/Shutterstock

LIBRARY OF CONGRESS CATALOGING-IN-PUBLICATION DATA

Names: Currie, Stephen, 1960- author.
Title: Systemic racism and the African American experience / Stephen Currie.
Description: San Diego : ReferencePoint Press, 2021. | Series: Being black in America | Includes bibliographical references and index.
Identifiers: LCCN 2020044942 (print) | LCCN 2020044943 (ebook) | ISBN 9781678200305 (library binding) | ISBN 9781678200312 (ebook)
Subjects: LCSH: Discrimination in criminal justice administration--United States--Juvenile literature. | Race discrimination--United States--Juvenile literature. | Racism--United States--Juvenile literature.
Classification: LCC HV9950 .C79 2021 (print) | LCC HV9950 (ebook) | DDC 364.3/496073--dc23
LC record available at https://lccn.loc.gov/2020044942
LC ebook record available at https://lccn.loc.gov/2020044943

CONTENTS

Introduction   4
  The Roots of Systemic Racism

Chapter One   8
  Health

Chapter Two   19
  Employment

Chapter Three   30
  Education

Chapter Four   42
  Policing and Incarceration

Source Notes   53
Organizations and Websites   58
For Further Research   60
Index   62

The Roots of Systemic Racism

For many years, it has been illegal for American landlords and real estate agents to discriminate against people on the basis of their race. But in early 2020 a group of researchers published a study demonstrating that discrimination in housing still exists. The study was carried out by Suffolk University Law School in Boston, Massachusetts, and its design was straightforward. Researchers began by asking Black and White "testers" to contact real estate agents, landlords, and property managers and to explain that they were looking for a place to live. Each agent or landlord was contacted by two testers—one Black and one White. The study aimed to see whether there were differences in how Blacks and Whites were treated in these circumstances.

Given the history of racism in the United States, the researchers were not surprised to find differences. They were shocked, however, to learn just how substantial those differences were. In most cases Black testers were treated significantly worse than their White counterparts.

For example, when White testers asked to see a particular apartment, 80 percent of their agents arranged to show them the property. In contrast, less than half the agents showed Black testers the rental units they wanted to see. Similarly, agents frequently offered White testers incentives to rent, such as monthly discounts and free parking; they rarely extended the same offers to Black testers. In all, the study concluded, 71 percent of agents showed clear bias against prospective customers who were Black. "This kind of discrimination is real," concludes William Berman, one of the researchers. "It's happening now in our community, and something needs to be done about it."[1]

The study in Boston is an example of systemic racism, also known as structural or institutional racism. When people think of racism, they often think of cruel and hurtful actions perpetrated by individual White people who have a deep dislike for Black people. There have been plenty of incidents in the United States that fit this description. But systemic racism is more subtle— and perhaps more widespread. In a way it can be seen as a collective racial prejudice, in which White people, often unwittingly, behave in ways that harm Black people. As the website Business Insider points out, systemic racism is "ingrained in nearly every way people move through society in the policies and practices at . . . banks, schools, companies, government agencies, and law enforcement."[2] In the Boston housing market, then, the issue is not just a handful of real estate agents who refuse to treat Blacks appropriately; the entire system of apartment hunting, in other words, involves racial bias.

> "This kind of discrimination is real. It's happening now in our community, and something needs to be done about it."[1]
>
> —William Berman, researcher

Racism and History

The roots of racism lie deep within American history. Indeed, racial discrimination has often been backed by laws designed to limit the freedoms and rights of African Americans. The institution of slavery, for example, made it entirely legal for one human being to own another—as long as the enslaved individual was Black. Following the Civil War and the abolition of slavery in the United States, White leaders created new laws that disadvantaged African Americans.

Research has shown that when Blacks search for a home to buy or rent, they experience worse treatment than their White counterparts receive.

These laws came to be known as Jim Crow laws, and they sharply limited the rights of Blacks. Most notably, Jim Crow laws segregated Blacks and Whites—that is, they kept the races apart in education, housing, and many other areas of life.

Legal slavery is long gone, and thanks to the civil rights movement of the 1950s and 1960s, legal segregation is also a thing of the past. But these earlier discriminatory laws continue to cast a shadow over race relations in the United States. Antiracism advocates point out that much of systemic racism is based on previous laws, particularly those from the Jim Crow era. Though these laws no longer exist, they still make up the foundation of biased practices and customs of today. In housing, for example, Jim Crow laws kept several generations of Blacks from moving into certain neighborhoods in many cities. While this type of segregation is no longer legal, the pattern of largely Black neighborhoods and heavily White neighborhoods persists.

Systemic racism also exists in large part because White people hold power in nearly all aspects of American life. The great bulk of landlords and real estate agents are white, for instance. So too are the majority of police chiefs, hiring managers, and college administrators. These White people have set up processes and systems that all too often advantage other Whites at the expense of Blacks. This bias may well be unconscious. But human psychology is complex, and it makes sense that real estate agents or hiring managers might be more welcoming to a person who looks like them and has a similar set of life experiences than to someone with a different racial background.

> "For far too many whites, if there is not a boogey man who can be pointed out and forced to apologize then racism doesn't exist."[3]
>
> —Mark Anthony Neal, professor at Duke University

Regardless of the reasons, there is little doubt that systemic racism is widespread within American society. From employment to health, and from policing to education, Blacks are frequently deprived of equal opportunities due to institutional bias. It is particularly difficult to end systemic racism because there is no single person who is obviously at fault; it can even be difficult to convince White people that systemic racism is real. "For far too many whites, if there is not a boogey man who can be pointed out and forced to apologize then racism doesn't exist,"[3] says Duke University professor Mark Anthony Neal. But the subtle nature of systemic racism makes it all the more pernicious—and all the more imperative that it be met head-on.

CHAPTER ONE

Health

Many families across America have been hit hard by the coronavirus pandemic of 2020, but few have been hit harder than the Fowler family of Detroit, Michigan. In the span of several hours in April 2020, David Fowler, age seventy-six, and his fifty-six-year-old son Gary both died of COVID-19. Gary's wife, Cheryl, also contracted COVID and spent several days on a ventilator shortly after the death of her husband, though the disease did not kill her. Two of the couple's adult children were diagnosed with COVID as well. Like their mother, they survived, but their experience with the disease was frightening. As a newspaper article puts it, the Fowlers were a family "ravaged by coronavirus."[4]

The Fowlers, who are African American, were appalled by how they were treated by hospital personnel. Recognizing that he was in serious condition and that his symptoms were consistent with COVID, Gary tried to check himself in to several different Detroit hospitals in the days before his death. But despite a high fever, a persistent cough, and shortness of breath, none of the hospitals admitted him as a patient. Fowler eventually gave up and returned home, where he died soon afterward. "He was begging for his life, and medical professionals did nothing for him,"[5] says Gary's stepson, Keith Gambrell.

Nor was Gary Fowler the only family member to receive substandard treatment. Gambrell recalls taking his mother to a local hospital just a few hours after her husband's death. "Before they even looked at my mother," Gambrell reports, "there was a young Caucasian lady complaining about sushi . . . that upset her stomach, and they swooped her in the back like she had coronavirus. But my mom, she had all the symptoms, and they [told] her just go home." Though Gambrell says he is not the sort of person who typically sees the world in racial terms, he admits it is difficult not to see racism in what happened to his family. "It's not right at all," he concludes. "When you see it, you have to call it how it is."[6]

Overall, in the United States the coronavirus has had a far greater impact on Black people than on White people. As of August 2020 the infection rate among Blacks was three times higher than the infection rate among Whites; thus, any given Black person is three times more likely to contract the disease compared to any given White person. The death rate of African Americans from COVID-19, likewise, is more than twice as high. These disparities are not rooted in random chance. On the contrary, the racial imbalance of COVID in America comes as no surprise to medical experts. One reason is institutional racism. "These racial [and] ethnic disparities in COVID-19 are the result of pre-pandemic realities," says Dr. Marcella Nunez-Smith of the Yale University School of Medicine. "It's a legacy of structural discrimination that has limited access to health and wealth for people of color."[7]

Indeed, COVID is just one of many diseases that strike Black Americans more often than White Americans. Cancer is more common among Blacks than Whites, for instance. So are strokes and chronic conditions such as asthma, diabetes, and high blood pressure. These conditions tend to be more serious, moreover, where African Americans are concerned. One possible consequence of diabetes, for instance, is the amputation of a leg or a foot, and Blacks are about two and a half times more likely than Whites to require this procedure. Another example is breast cancer, which kills women of all races—but according to the Centers for Disease Control and Prevention (CDC), the death rate among Black women with the disease is 40 percent higher than the rate among White women. The CDC also notes that Blacks die earlier than Whites, and they have a lower quality of life measured

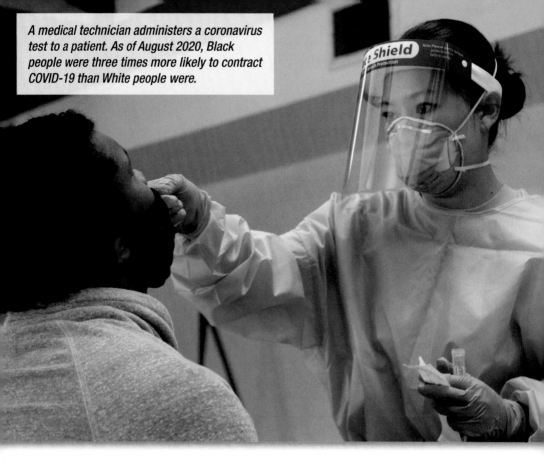

A medical technician administers a coronavirus test to a patient. As of August 2020, Black people were three times more likely to contract COVID-19 than White people were.

by almost any medical yardstick. From this perspective, the high COVID-related death rate among African Americans was depressingly easy to anticipate.

Valuing Patients

As Nunez-Smith points out, many of the reasons for the gaps in medical outcomes lie in systemic racism. In some cases, the issues are easy to see. Keith Gambrell's difficulty in getting care for his mother is a clear example: in his view, hospital staff seemed more interested in assisting a White person than an African American, even though the Black patient was suffering from a much more serious—and indeed, deadly—condition. Faced with patients of two races, hospital employees seemed to believe that the White patient was of more value than the Black one. Certainly, that is a textbook definition of racism.

Gambrell's suspicions, moreover, are borne out by research. One recent study, for instance, tracked how long it took for White and Black patients to be seen at emergency rooms. The results revealed that White patients typically spend eighty minutes waiting for care and receiving services. The corresponding figure for Blacks, in contrast, is ninety-nine minutes—nearly 25 percent longer. The authors of the study note that some of the disparity may relate to the number of patients in any given emergency room but believe the primary reason involves racism. Others agree. "It could be bias, conscious or unconscious, on the part of providers or other staff that work at the site where they're receiving care,"[8] says Alexander Green, a doctor at Massachusetts General Hospital.

Statistics also bear out the claim that Blacks receive less effective care than Whites for their medical issues. That is particularly true where preventive care is concerned. "Black patients are 10 percent less likely to be screened for high cholesterol than white Americans," writes physician Robert Pearl. "The result is higher rates of heart failure and strokes for African Americans."[9] White women are more likely than Black women to get screenings for breast cancer, too. Diabetes is another example. Research shows that White patients with diabetes typically are diagnosed sooner than Black patients with diabetes.

And the way doctors respond to Blacks and Whites is often different as well. Treatment for breast cancer, for example, may involve a mastectomy—the removal of one or both breasts. Doctors try to avoid this outcome if at all possible, yet they apparently try harder when patients are White. According to researchers at the University of Pennsylvania, mastectomies are more common for Black women than for White women. Many studies have noted that doctors take complaints of pain from patients more seriously when the patients are White than when they

> "Black patients are 10 percent less likely to be screened for high cholesterol than white Americans. The result is higher rates of heart failure and strokes for African Americans."[9]
>
> —Robert Pearl, physician

are Black. A 2016 report in the *Journal of American Medicine* revealed that even among children, those who are Black receive less treatment for pain. There are discrepancies, too, as people approach death. "Physicians generally interact less—both verbally and nonverbally—with black patients who are dying than with white patients who are dying," reports Yolonda Wilson, a professor at Howard University. "At the end of their lives, black patients do not receive the same comfort care, including eye contact and touch, from physicians that white patients do."[10]

Other research also points to unconscious racism on the part of medical personnel in creating the disparities between White and Black medical outcomes. Green once designed a study of emergency room physicians to determine the degree of racial bias

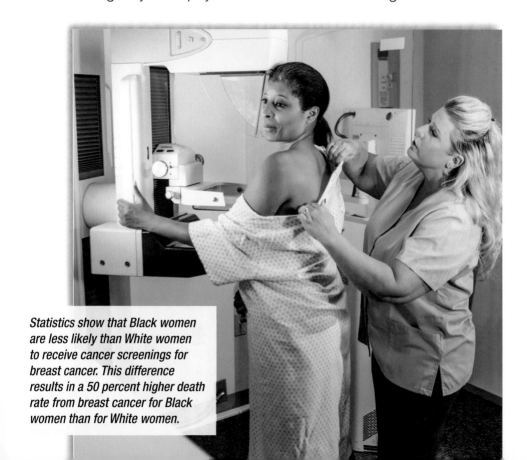

Statistics show that Black women are less likely than White women to receive cancer screenings for breast cancer. This difference results in a 50 percent higher death rate from breast cancer for Black women than for White women.

toward patients. He gave doctors a medical chart of a patient suffering chest pains and asked the doctors to recommend a course of treatment. Green included photos with the chart showing the supposed face of the patient. Half the doctors saw a photo of a Black person, the other half a photo of a White person. Green discovered that doctors who believed the patient was Black recommended less aggressive treatment—treatments less likely to result in a positive outcome for the patient—than doctors who believed the patient was White.

Money, Insurance, and Health Care

At heart, the systemic racism in health care stems from the realities of American life. The issue of money, for example, looms over any discussion of health care and race. As a group, Blacks have always been significantly poorer than Whites, and that disparity persists today. Most obviously, as of 2020 the median income of African American families is about half the median income of White families. But Blacks are also less likely to have significant assets such as homes, stocks, and pension plans, and the value of the assets they hold is considerably less. By some estimates, the typical White family has ten times more wealth than the typical Black family.

Because health care is expensive, this gap has an enormous impact on the health of Black Americans. Many low-wage workers, especially in certain states, do not qualify for government assistance with health insurance. At the same time, they find private plans unaffordable. The high rate of poverty among African Americans thus means that Blacks are more likely to be uninsured than Whites. Indeed, as of 2020 fully a quarter of American Blacks lacked health insurance. For want of insurance, Black people often put off getting routine medical care and ignore more significant medical conditions. The relative lack of wealth among Black families—a reality produced by generations of racial bias—has made it difficult for Blacks to obtain health insurance, with dire consequences for their well-being.

The issues with insurance also affect poor Blacks who do qualify for government-sponsored programs such as Medicare or Medicaid. In wealthy, heavily White communities, hospitals generally are reimbursed the full cost of treatments from their patients' private insurance companies. The same is not true for so-called safety net hospitals, which typically treat poorer patients on government plans and are often located in Black neighborhoods. Unlike private insurers, the government does not fully reimburse hospitals for these patients. That discrepancy cuts into the hospital's income. And the hospital bears the entire cost of treatment for patients without health insurance at all. Hospitals in low-income, heavily Black communities therefore experience chronic financial difficulties. Many have closed, thus reducing the health care options for neighborhood residents. "In an instance where a safety net hospital goes out of business," points out Thomas LaVeist, a professor at Tulane University, "the health needs of the community don't disappear."[11]

Again, the COVID crisis points up these disparities. Socioeconomic factors such as income and education help explain why Blacks' infection and death rates for COVID are so high. People who work in lower-wage and lower-skilled jobs find it more difficult to social distance or to work from home than people in higher socioeconomic levels. Because African Americans typically have less education and less family wealth than Whites, they are more likely to work in jobs that carry a higher risk of contracting the coronavirus. Moreover, they are more likely to take public transportation to work and to live in crowded apartment buildings. "Can you possibly take an elevator alone?" asks epidemiologist Martina Anto-Ocrah, speaking of people living in low-income housing complexes. "No."[12] The social and economic circumstances of Black life in the United States thus help explain why Blacks have been so severely affected by COVID.

However, a lack of money does not explain all the discrepancies between Black and White patients. Blacks who

> **"Can you possibly take an elevator alone? No."[12]**
>
> —Martina Anto-Ocrah, epidemiologist

Computers, Health Care, and Racism

Much about patient care today is left to computers. Using an algorithm, or a series of steps, computers will take information about a patient and his or her symptoms, apply the steps, and report what the program sees as the best treatment. Unfortunately, recent research has indicated that the algorithms used by many hospitals and insurance companies are racially biased. Computers running these algorithms routinely recommend more aggressive treatments for Whites than for Blacks. The main reason for this discrepancy involves the way the algorithms are set up. One piece of information they use is the amount of money spent on a patient's health care during the previous year. The more money, the more aggressive the recommended treatment; the algorithm assumes that more money equates to a sicker patient.

However, where race is concerned that is inaccurate. In fact, White patients are more likely to see a doctor when they are sick. Studies show that total spending for a Black patient is about $1,800 a year less than a White patient who is equally sick. "Black people," a journalist concludes, "had to be sicker than white people before being referred for additional help." Even a computer program, it seems, can be biased.

Heidi Ledford, "Millions of Black People Affected by Racial Bias in Health-Care Algorithms," *Nature*, October 24, 2019. www.nature.com.

enjoy higher social status, educational levels, and income do not automatically receive medical treatment on a par with Whites. Joneigh Khaldun, a Black physician who runs the Detroit Health Department, experienced racial discrimination firsthand soon after she gave birth. "I'm a doctor," she says, "and my own doctor did not listen to my concerns about a headache when I had my first child. And I ended up in an ICU [intensive care unit] with a head full of blood."[13] Even medical professionals who are Black cannot count on being taken seriously by their physicians. Systemic racism does not affect only the poor and less well educated.

Looking Ahead

Fixing the institutional racism in the American health care system will not be easy. One potentially useful strategy would be to change the way health insurance works in this country. Two-time presidential candidate Bernie Sanders, among others, has advocated for a "Medicare for all" system in which tax money funds a government-sponsored health insurance plan for all Americans. Under this plan, private insurance companies would be eliminated. Others suggest a more measured approach in which cheap government plans would be available to anyone who wants them, but private insurance would still be obtainable by those who prefer it. By ensuring that everyone can be covered by a low-cost health plan, these suggestions would certainly help the 25 percent of Black people who currently lack health insurance of any kind.

However, there is strong opposition to these plans. Many conservatives have resisted efforts to expand government-sponsored health care, believing that the cost to taxpayers will

Socioeconomic factors such as education and income mean that Blacks are more likely than Whites to rely on public transportation for commuting, which increases the risk of contracting the coronavirus.

Blacks and COVID-19 Testing

Despite the high coronavirus infection rates for Blacks, African Americans as a group tend to be given fewer tests for the disease. One reason for this is that most testing sites are set up for vehicles: people seeking tests drive into a testing site and are given a COVID test without leaving their cars. This process is convenient for drivers as well as medical staff, and it helps reduce the risk of contagion, but it does have one drawback: it only works for people who have vehicles.

Because Blacks tend to be poorer than Whites and because they are more likely to live in urban regions and be dependent on public transportation, African Americans are less likely to own cars. Indeed, one study found that one in five African American families has no access to a car, while the same is true for just one White family in twenty. Thus, Black families are less likely to be able to access COVID testing. This is yet another example of systemic racism. No one intended that Blacks be denied coronavirus tests—but that was an inadvertent consequence of an otherwise reasonable policy.

be too high and instead supporting private plans. "Medicare for all is a terrible idea," says Michigan politician John James. "We can barely pay for Medicare for some."[14] Moreover, structural racism is not just about health insurance: It is also about taking Black patients' complaints less seriously, requiring African Americans to wait longer for treatment, and giving them less thorough care than White patients receive. To truly eradicate institutional racism in the health care system will require major changes in how health care providers think.

Since health care workers often harbor unconscious prejudices against African Americans, that most likely means education. Medical workers must first be aware of the biases they have before they can overcome them. Thus, some experts and groups are calling for racism-awareness training for doctors, nurses, and other medical personnel. "We call on medical institutions and associations to require implicit bias training for all health care workers, including as part of initial and ongoing medical certification,"[15] write three physicians in an article appearing in *Scientific American*. Indeed, California has already mandated this type of training for people involved in perinatal care—that is, the care given during the weeks immediately before and after birth.

And some medical workers are reaching into Black neighborhoods in an attempt to lessen the impact of structural racism in the health care system. In Detroit, for example, medical professionals are working with community organizations to raise awareness of high blood pressure—a condition that affects many Blacks. Some of the outreach focuses on peer-to-peer education, in which Blacks who are not medical workers are given information about blood pressure control and then deputized to spread the word among their families and friends. Such programs provide Blacks with information they need—but away from the hospitals and doctors' offices where systemic racism is all too frequent.

The racism in the American health care system may be difficult to solve, but leaving it to flourish is not an option. It is imperative that Blacks be treated fairly and respectfully by doctors, nurses, and other medical personnel. That means valuing the life of a Black patient just as much as the life of a White patient. It means extending treatments commonly used on White patients to Black patients as well. And it means being aware of the subtle racial biases that medical workers often bring to their jobs—and being willing to move beyond them. Only then will our health care system be one that works on behalf of all people regardless of race.

CHAPTER TWO

Employment

The great majority of players in the National Football League (NFL) are Black. But an even greater majority of the people who run the teams are not. Each of the league's thirty-two teams has a head coach, who motivates the players, runs practices, and takes charge of strategy during the games. As of September 2020 just three of those thirty-two head coaches were African American. For would-be coaching candidates, journalist Dave Zirin observes drily, "whiteness appears to be a necessary precondition to finding work."[16] Each team also has a general manager, whose duties include choosing the players who make up the team's roster. African American general managers are even rarer than Black head coaches: in 2020 the Miami Dolphins' Chris Grier was the only Black general manager in the league.

Some observers do not see a problem with this situation. To them, the lack of Black head coaches and general managers simply means that there were more qualified White candidates for these positions. "We're a league of meritocracy," says Denver Broncos coach Vic Fangio. "You earn what you get, you get what you earn."[17] But an increasing number of players, fans, and journalists say otherwise. When one head coaching vacancy after another goes to a White person—often chosen over an extremely well-qualified Black candidate—the pattern becomes difficult to ignore. In effect, critics say, the NFL is limiting the roles Black people may have within the league. Teams are happy to hire Black men to play the games but are not eager to fill management roles with African Americans.

This reality has prompted charges of institutional racism. Whether NFL leaders intended it or not, the league has established a system in which Blacks have little chance to be hired for a position of authority. The hiring of a succession of White candidates to be coaches and general managers is evidently not based entirely on merit. Rather, racial discrimination, however subtle, is at work. "This is what systemic racism looks like," writes journalist Dave Fymbo, referring specifically to the scarcity of Black head coaches in the league. "It is not a single hiring choice that you can point to. It is a system run by white owners that favors white coaches."[18]

> "This is what systemic racism looks like. It is not a single hiring choice that you can point to. It is a system run by white owners that favors white coaches."[18]
>
> —Dave Fymbo, journalist

The institutional racism many see in the NFL is reflected in employment issues elsewhere in society. African Americans in the workplace are subject to discrimination in a variety of industries and in a variety of ways. This takes place both on the job and while searching for employment. They are the last to be hired and the first to be laid off; their pay is lower than the pay of their White colleagues; and they are seldom offered high-paying, high-status jobs even when they are well qualified. In few areas of American life is systemic racism as damaging as it is in employment.

Unemployment and Job Searches

Statistics make it clear that systemic racism is a significant problem where jobs are concerned. According to the Bureau of Labor Statistics, for instance, Black people are nearly twice as likely as White people to be unemployed. In 2010, as the United States was coming out of a recession, about 9 percent of White people were unemployed, but the rate for Blacks was 17 percent. In 2020, shortly before the coronavirus pandemic arrived, unemployment rates had fallen for both groups but remained higher for African Americans, 6 percent to 3 percent. The widespread loss of jobs once the pandemic began also affected Blacks more than Whites. "Fewer than half of all Black Americans had a job in April and May [2020],"[19] notes Business Insider.

While unemployment affects Blacks at all wage and salary levels, research shows that Blacks have particular difficulty finding work in professional fields—relatively high-paying jobs such as management, nursing, and engineering. A recent study by a federal agency found that 41 percent of White workers held jobs in a professional field, compared to only 31 percent of Blacks. And at the highest salary levels, Blacks are almost nonexistent. As of August 2020 Black executives ran just three of the five hundred wealthiest companies in the United States. "It's embarrassing," says Kenneth Chenault, who once led financial services corporation American Express. "There are thousands of black people

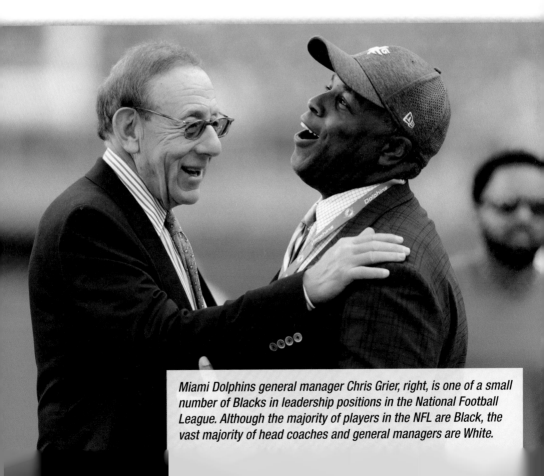

Miami Dolphins general manager Chris Grier, right, is one of a small number of Blacks in leadership positions in the National Football League. Although the majority of players in the NFL are Black, the vast majority of head coaches and general managers are White.

who are just as qualified or more qualified than I am who deserve the opportunity, but haven't been given the opportunity."[20]

One reason for the discrepancy in employment involves the way that employers fill job vacancies. Today job openings are nearly always posted on the internet. "I found my job online," says Philadelphia resident Caitlin Day. "I arranged my interview online, and I interviewed online."[21] Day is not alone. A 2019 study revealed that 41 percent of successful job applicants used the internet to find their new jobs, and experts agree that this figure will increase in the future. However, the shift to online job searches has not benefited all workers equally. Some people have easy access to the internet while others do not, a phenomenon known as the digital divide. On one side of the divide, millions of Americans take internet access for granted. On the other, millions more have limited access at best.

Several factors, including geography and income, play a role in the digital divide. But race is an important factor as well. A Pew Research Center study from 2019, for example, revealed that 82 percent of White Americans own a computer, compared to just 58 percent of Blacks. Similarly, Whites are more likely than Blacks to own smartphones or to have broadband internet access at home. For many Blacks, the internet is only available through public computers at libraries or community centers—a much less convenient and reliable method of access than having a secure connection at home. With so many jobs being posted online, Black job seekers frequently have difficulty learning about possible employment opportunities.

The great majority of businesses use online postings because the internet is efficient and quick. In general, companies have learned that posting job vacancies on the internet is an excellent way to attract well-qualified candidates. Their goal is to widen

Job openings are often posted online, but a lower rate of computer ownership places Blacks at a disadvantage compared to their White counterparts in searching for employment.

their applicant pool, not to exclude possible African American applicants. But the system of posting job vacancies online has the effect of limiting the number of Black candidates. This unwitting discrimination against Black job seekers is an excellent example of institutional racism. Until the digital divide disappears, many African Americans will be excluded from large sections of the job market.

Networking and Stereotypes

Online postings are not the only way for job seekers to find work. Many people get their jobs through a process known as networking—that is, forming relationships with people who work in similar fields. People looking for jobs can ask others in their network whether they know of companies that are hiring. "Locate friends and contacts who are connected to the company where you want to work," advises an article in the business-oriented *Forbes* magazine. "Reach out to those contacts through personalized emails and phone calls. Ask if you can mention them in an email or call to your target."[22]

Black Executives and Diversity

Research shows that Black executives often do not extend themselves to help younger, lower-ranking African Americans. There are good reasons for this: although younger Blacks would certainly benefit from having a same-race mentor and role model, the risk for a high-status Black worker is high. When high-ranking Blacks do advocate for other Blacks, they may be seen as focused entirely on racial politics rather than having the good of the company in mind. This can cause the Black employee to lose status in the eyes of his or her coworkers. In one study Blacks who were especially vocal about hiring other Blacks were less respected by their peers than Blacks who were more muted in their support.

Moreover, Black executives are sometimes accused of reverse racism simply for trying to diversify their work force. "Sam's Club is anti-White," one Twitter user wrote angrily when Sam's Club executive Rosalind Brewer called for more diversity in hiring at her company. "Boycott them." Of course, Brewer was not telling managers at Sam's Club to stop hiring White people, but that was how some of her company's customers interpreted her words. These are the pitfalls faced by powerful Blacks in the business world if they choose to support diversity or other Black workers.

Quoted in Sara Ashley, "Sam's Club CEO Takes Heat for Diversity Comments," CNN, December 16, 2015. https://money.cnn.com.

Networking can certainly be a powerful tool for job seekers. The phrase "it's not what you know, it's who you know" is common in the business world, and there is plenty of truth in it. Though estimates vary widely, most experts agree that over half of all new employees get their jobs at least in part through networking. Indeed, in some cases networking is absolutely essential to finding employment. Quite a few jobs—including some very high-profile executive positions—are poorly advertised or not advertised at all. Managers at these companies often form an applicant pool from among people they already know and then hire someone within that network.

But just as online applications often put Black people at a disadvantage, networking can have the same result. While there are certainly exceptions, many Americans do not establish close relationships with people of other races. According to one study, about 75 percent of Whites admit to having no non-White friends. That is an issue because Whites hold most positions of power and authority. When a new position opens up at a business, White managers who participate in networking tend to hire other White people. "Caucasian men use their power at work to refer more Caucasian men for jobs,"[23] concludes a report from the American Bar Association, a lawyers' organization.

Like online job searching, networking thus has the effect of making it more difficult for Black workers to find employment. At worst, networking can exclude Black workers altogether. Black people may still benefit from networking with other Blacks—but networking is most effective when it is done with people in high-ranking positions in companies and organizations. Since African Americans less often hold positions of authority, opportunities for this type of networking may be limited. "Those who are not part of the networks of people who can help you find a job are at a major disadvantage,"[24] says Rutgers University professor Nancy DiTomaso. That disadvantage will fade once more African Americans hold positions of authority in US businesses.

> "Caucasian men use their power at work to refer more Caucasian men for jobs."[23]
>
> —American Bar Association

Another issue, primarily affecting Black people at the professional level, involves stereotyping. Whether they are aware of it or not, most people have a mental image of what a scientist, a business executive, or a school principal looks like. In many cases the image that immediately comes to mind is a person who is White. In contrast, when people think of a lower-status occupation such as home health care aide, they often picture a person of color.

There is evidence that African Americans may suffer in the job market because of these stereotypes. A hiring committee may have difficulty envisioning a Black person as a lawyer, a professor, or an engineer and may give the job to a White candidate instead.

Income

Finding jobs is not the only way in which Black workers are disadvantaged. Earnings are another. There are significant differences in what companies pay their White and Black employees. In 2019 the average Black worker earned about sixty-two cents for every dollar earned by the average White worker—and that gap has been slowly widening over time. Some of that disparity is because Whites tend to work in more lucrative occupations. But even when Blacks and Whites perform the same work and hold the same qualifications, Whites earn more than their Black colleagues. "After controlling for age, gender, education, and region," writes economist Elise Gould, "black workers are paid 14.9% less than white workers."[25] This difference is the result of racial discrimination.

The wage disparity prevails across all educational levels. Among workers who never finished high school, Whites outearn Blacks by more than two dollars an hour. The gap grows as educational attainment rises. Among those with advanced degrees, the difference is more than six dollars an hour. Sometimes the disparity is significantly greater than that. One Black man, identified in a news article only as Bryan, made an unpleasant discovery after reaching a high-profile position within a large corporation. "I learned I was being paid less than half of what my white colleagues earned," he explains. "When I confronted [the human resources department] and my manager about it, they blatantly lied to me."[26] Bryan eventually left his job.

Much of the reason for the wage gap lies with the companies doing the hiring. "Black job seekers were offered significantly less compensation than whites by potential new employers,"[27] concludes one study of unemployed workers in New Jersey. Once

Some anti-racism advocates say that the process of recruiting and interviewing job applicants is flawed, resulting in a lack of diversity among workers.

Black applicants accepted that lower salary, they were likely to continue making less than their White coworkers, as future raises would be based on these initial earnings. Even if they moved to a different company, the new employer was likely to ask them about their salary history—their earnings with their former employer—meaning that Black workers would again be at a disadvantage. As financial adviser Shahar Ziv puts it, "Salary histories enable a form of institutional discrimination. Even if employers do not individually discriminate, the use of salary histories appears to perpetuate the effects of past discrimination or other group inequities."[28]

The Future

As with health care, ending systemic racism in employment is not going to be an easy task. Nevertheless, people are trying to reduce the effects of structural racism with the hope of eventually ending it altogether. Ziv, for example, suggests that one way forward is for employers to stop asking about salary history. Ideally, he would

Jobs and the Coronavirus

One reason why COVID-19 especially affects Black people involves the realities of the workplace. As reporter Steven Greenhouse described it in an article published in July 2020:

> A disproportionate percentage of Black people hold jobs that make them essential workers. Blacks represent 11.9 per cent of the total workforce, but they make up 14.2 per cent of the workforce at grocery, convenience, and drug stores; twenty-six per cent in public transit; 18.2 per cent in trucking, warehouse, and mail service; 17.5 per cent in health care; and 19.3 per cent in child care and social services. Essential workers often say that they are not adequately protected. In April, Maya Smith, an African-American cashier at a Walmart in New Orleans, told New Orleans Public Radio that her boss didn't allow workers to wear masks, because some shoppers thought it meant the workers were infected, and Jennifer Suggs, an African-American Walmart cashier in South Carolina, said, "We're not essential. We're sacrificial. I will be replaced if I die from this. I don't have a mask or gloves. The only thing I have is a stupid blue vest."

Steven Greenhouse, "The Coronavirus Pandemic Has Intensified Systemic Economic Racism Against Black Americans," *New Yorker*, July 30, 2020. www.newyorker.com.

like a nationwide ban on the practice. Short of that, he suggests that individual corporations mandate an end to asking about salary history. Rather than just talking about change, he writes, "It would be a concrete action that they could take."[29] Indeed, several states and municipalities have recently passed laws to prevent employers from inquiring about salary history. While these laws are designed more to protect women than to protect people of color, there is no question that they benefit Black people as well—and help eliminate at least one aspect of systemic racism.

As for what can be done on the job, some experts see value in communication. "Oppose discrimination and racism in all of its forms," a law firm in California advises workers. "If you notice Black job candidates are being repeatedly passed over, report it to management, in writing."[30] Communicating in writing, the firm notes, helps managers see the seriousness of the problem—and makes it more difficult for them to ignore what is going on. Others say that simply listening to Black workers' experiences can go a long way toward reducing racism.

Changing some aspects of job hunting may also make a difference. Some antiracism advocates focus on the process of recruiting and interviewing candidates. It is tempting for business owners to hire from among people they already know, for example, but doing so tends to perpetuate systemic racism. "Cast the net wide so you're not always recruiting from the same narrow pool of candidates,"[31] advises a publication aimed at small businesses. Another suggestion involves what happens when the list of candidates has been winnowed down to three or four. If all those candidates are White, antiracist leaders suggest, then the process may have been flawed and should be reviewed for hidden bias.

> "If you notice Black job candidates are being repeatedly passed over, report it to management, in writing."[30]
>
> —California law firm Levy Vinick Burrell Hyams

Systemic racism, in short, is everywhere in employment. Though American companies often make diversity one of their central goals—businesses collectively spend billions of dollars on diversity programs every year—the reality is very different. Companies with initiatives encouraging Blacks to apply often undermine these efforts by posting job vacancies only online or by filling jobs based mainly on managerial networks. And even businesses that strive to pay African Americans as much as Whites often fail to reach this standard. In every way, Blacks are victims of discrimination in the job market and at work. Ending this systemic racism in employment will be one of the biggest tasks for society in the years ahead.

CHAPTER THREE

Education

The public school system in Charlottesville, Virginia, reflects the city's overall diversity. About 40 percent of Charlottesville's students are White, and about 30 percent of the student body is African American. But though the numbers are roughly equal, the experiences of the two groups are not. While the typical White student in Charlottesville reads at or above grade level, for instance, the average Black student does not. For every Black student in the district's gifted and talented program, there are three White students. And Black students in Charlottesville are more likely than White students to be held back a grade, more likely to be suspended, and less likely to be placed into advanced courses. "I know what I'm capable of and what I can do," says 2019 district graduate Trinity Hughes, an African American who was kept out of high-level classes, "but the counselors and teachers, they don't really care about that."[32]

Charlottesville is not unusual in these respects. In schools across the country, Black students' test scores and graduation rates lag behind those of their White counterparts. Similarly, Black students nationally are more often in trouble than their White classmates. Some observers take this data to mean that Black students, as a group, are poorly prepared for school and unwilling or unable to control their behavior. But most experts say the situation is not that simple. Instead, they point out that the country's educational system, especially at the kindergarten through twelfth-grade levels, is set up in ways that subtly favor White students over their Black counterparts. Proponents of this perspective point to differences in funding for schools according to their racial makeup, differing expectations for students of varying racial backgrounds, and other issues to bolster their contention that systemic racism is at the heart of what makes Black students struggle.

Segregation and Funding

One of the most obvious examples of systemic racism in education involves segregation, or the separation of students according to race. Until 1954 segregation was perfectly legal—and very common. Hundreds of communities, especially in the South, had schools that were open only to Whites and others that were attended exclusively by Blacks. Though in theory the schools offered identical programs, in practice the Black schools were underfunded and poorly equipped in comparison to the White schools. "We didn't have a gym at all," recalls Charles Coward, who graduated from all-Black Adkin High in Kinston, North Carolina, during the early 1950s. "We didn't have a proper cafeteria. . . . [The school board] never had money for the black schools."[33]

In 1954, however, the US Supreme Court ruled unanimously in a case known as *Brown v. Board of Education* that the segregation of schools was unconstitutional. As Chief Justice Earl Warren put it, "Separate educational facilities are inherently unequal."[34] The *Brown* case was groundbreaking in that it affirmed the rights of Blacks and the equality of all Americans regardless of race. But in the nearly seventy years since the decision was handed down, its goals have proved elusive. Even today, thousands of schools across the country remain sharply divided according to race. More than half of American public school students live in districts where the student body is at least 75 percent White or 75 percent non-White. Many schools are virtually 100 percent Black; many more are close to 100 percent White.

> **"I know what I'm capable of and what I can do, but the counselors and teachers, they don't really care about that."[32]**
>
> —Trinity Hughes, high school graduate in Charlottesville, Virginia

The disparities matter. Most obviously, heavily Black schools receive considerably less funding than do predominately White schools. In 2019, for example, schools with high White populations received over $2,200 more per student than schools with high non-White populations. Income is one reason for the disparity, of course. School districts with mainly Black students tend to serve a high proportion of students from poor families, limiting the amount of money a district can get from local taxes. But even when the income of district residents is identical, schools with large Black populations suffer compared to their White counterparts. As journalist Clare Lombardo summarizes, "High-poverty districts serving mostly students of color receive about $1,600 less per student than the national average . . . while school districts that are predominately white and poor receive about $130 less."[35]

And money makes an enormous difference in education. With an extra $2,200 per student, a largely White district can hire more experienced and effective teachers and administrators than a Black district can afford. Alternatively, that money can replace crumbling school buildings, reduce the student-to-teacher ratio, and help purchase state-of-the-art technology. All of these expenditures have an important effect on student achievement as measured by standardized test scores, college admission rates, and other yardsticks. The graduation rate for high school students in Scarsdale, New York, a district that spends far more per student than almost any other in the nation, is above 99 percent. "Increased school spending improves student outcomes,"[36] sums up economics professor Kirabo Jackson.

Black Children and Preschool

At first glance, early childhood education seems remarkably free of racism. Head Start, a well-known early childhood program funded by the government, enrolls a greater percentage of Black students than White students. Research suggests, moreover, that Head Start does an excellent job of preparing children for the public school system. "Head Start improves children's educational outcomes," writes Christine Johnson-Staub of the Center for Law and Social Policy, "increasing the chances that participants graduate from high school and complete postsecondary education and training." Indeed, Johnson-Staub notes, the outcomes for Black students tend to be especially strong.

Nonetheless, structural racism is present even at the preschool level. According to the civil rights division of the US Department of Education, African Americans make up 48 percent of preschoolers who are suspended from school more than once—yet they account for just 18 percent of all preschool students. Access to quality childcare programs is another problem. Many Black parents work evening, night, or weekend shifts, when many care centers are closed. "Head Start preschool and pre-kindergarten programs are only available during traditional hours," observes Johnson-Staub. While Black children whose parents work during the day can attend these programs, many more cannot—and therefore cannot benefit from them.

Christine Johnson-Staub, "Equity Starts Early," Center for Law and Social Policy, 2017. www.clasp.org.

Conversely, the lack of money causes many largely Black districts to struggle to educate their students. Tales abound of heavily minority schools lacking guidance counselors, library books, and other important resources. "In Bridgeport, where class sizes hover near the contractual maximum of 29, students use 15- to 20-year-old textbooks," writes journalist Alana Semuels in a survey of impoverished Connecticut school districts. "In New London, high-school teachers must duct tape windows shut to keep out the wind and snow and station trash cans in the hallways to collect rain."[37] These conditions are not conducive to learning, and the results are predictable. Heavily Black schools are all too often characterized by low test scores, high dropout rates, and an overall lack of student achievement. This is one effect of the systemic racism that pushes Black students into schools that struggle to meet their needs.

Until 1954, racial segregation in schools was both legal and common. Although in theory all schools were equal, in reality Black schools were underfunded and poorly equipped in comparison to White schools.

Attendance Zones

On one level, segregated schools are simply the result of geography. As former New York City mayor Michael Bloomberg argues, "For far too long, zip code and skin color have determined a child's education."[38] Simply put, Blacks tend to live in certain towns, cities, and neighborhoods, while Whites typically settle in different areas. This process is known as housing segregation, and school attendance areas frequently are based on the boundaries between these communities. Students in one development, neighborhood, or village attend one school, while those just a mile or so away attend another. The racial makeup of schools thus reflects the often-segregated demographics of the communities they serve.

> **"For far too long, zip code and skin color have determined a child's education."[38]**
>
> —Michael Bloomberg, former New York City mayor

The situation is perhaps most obvious where school district boundaries are concerned. The Poughkeepsie City School District in Poughkeepsie, New York, for instance, is heavily minority. The student body at the district's high school is 57 percent Black, with most of the remainder being Hispanic. Just to the south of Poughkeepsie lies the Spackenkill district, a majority White district in which only 12 percent of the students are Black. Despite their proximity, the demographics of the two communities are very different, and that difference is reflected in the racial breakdown of the school systems as well. Unsurprisingly, Spackenkill outranks Poughkeepsie in every measure of school success. Similar pairs of adjacent school districts can be found across most of the country.

However, even within school districts, racial imbalances are common. In Charlottesville, for instance, children living in heavily Black neighborhoods on the south side of town typically are drawn into majority-Black elementary schools, while children in low-minority neighborhoods on the city's north side more often attend elementary schools with majority White populations. In

Standardized Testing

Standardized tests are a common feature in American education. From third-grade reading tests to college admission exams, these tests are designed to rank students from many different schools and educational backgrounds. Many people, even many educators, believe that these tests should be unbiased. But in fact they are not, to the detriment of Black students everywhere. Black students typically score much lower than White students on these kinds of tests. This is true regardless of socioeconomic status: that is, even well-off Black students, on average, do worse than equally well-off White students.

This matters because standardized testing is used in many aspects of education. Lower SAT and ACT scores can make it more difficult for Black students to get into college—especially high-prestige and more selective colleges. Standardized test scores also contribute to the large number of African American children shunted into remedial learning classes. And in some cities, such as Philadelphia and Chicago, low standardized test scores have been used as a justification to close heavily Black schools rather than to improve the quality of the education the schools provide. In all these ways standardized testing contributes to the racism prevalent in the educational system.

the school district that serves Wake County, North Carolina, high schools range from 67 percent Black to almost 75 percent White. Again, geography makes the difference; Blacks and Whites are not evenly distributed across the county, and as a result different high schools in the region frequently serve very different communities.

Often, the boundaries that form school attendance areas are themselves examples of systemic racism. In many cases Blacks have been excluded from certain neighborhoods or towns, whether due to income or by being made to feel unwelcome. Since Blacks typically have less wealth than Whites, they may not be able to afford to live in some well-off towns, especially certain suburbs of large cities. The boundaries are self-perpetuating, too—that is, a district that is heavily Black tends to remain so as White families avoid moving into the district. "Many white families in America," writes journalist Alvin Chang, "want to live in a certain type of community and want their kids to be educated in a certain type of school."[39] Whether they admit it or not, that type of school often includes few Black children. This, too, shows institutional racism at work.

In some places, moreover, there have been deliberate attempts to further segregate schools by shifting district boundaries. One example is Shelby County, Tennessee, a school district that at one point included both the city of Memphis and many of its suburbs. In 2014 six of those suburbs broke away from the Shelby County district to form their own districts. The schools remaining in the Shelby County district are about 79 percent Black, while the new districts are much more heavily White: Collierville High School in one of these new districts, for example, is just 19 percent African American. The secession of districts sparked intense criticism among many residents of the city of Memphis. "You're thriving because due to white privilege you removed yourself from the 'urban' district," points out activist Tami Sawyer, speaking to White parents living in the suburban areas. "This is racially motivated and wrong."[40]

Discipline and Remediation

Even in relatively diverse schools and school districts, systemic racism remains a problem. One way to measure institutional racism involves school discipline. Many schools use out-of-school suspension as a punishment for serious misbehavior. The number of suspensions is tracked by the federal government, which breaks down suspensions by race, among other categories. As of 2020 about 13 percent of Black students are suspended at some point during the school year—a figure more than twice as high as the corresponding percentage of White students. The disparity is even greater for expulsions, an even more severe penalty:

Black students are three times more likely to be expelled from a public school than are White students.

Many observers attribute the high rate of suspensions and expulsions to unconscious racism on the part of teachers and administrators. There is evidence that Black and White children are not punished equally for the same offenses. A Black child who is disruptive may be suspended, while a White child doing exactly the same thing is merely scolded. There is also evidence that White adults view Black children differently from White children. In particular, Black children are often viewed as older than their actual ages, which means they are more likely to be held accountable for their poor behavior. According to researcher Phillip Goff, "Black boys can be seen as responsible for their actions at an age when white boys still benefit from the assumption that children are essentially innocent."[41]

Institutional racism also appears within individual schools. The situation in Charlottesville, where gifted classes and advanced courses are populated largely by White students, is repeated across much of the United States. Researcher Kayla Patrick has found, for example, that African Americans make up just 9 percent of students in Advanced Placement classes nationally, as opposed to 15 percent of students overall. At the same time, Blacks make up a disproportionately large share of students assigned to remedial classes. "If you walk into your average high school," says Patrick, "you might see diverse hallways but not diverse classrooms."[42] Again, Black students are shortchanged by this type of systemic racism.

> "Black boys can be seen as responsible for their actions at an age when white boys still benefit from the assumption that children are essentially innocent."[41]
>
> —Phillip Goff, researcher

Colleges and Universities

Most of the attention paid to systemic racism in education focuses on K–12 schools. But institutional racism is prevalent at

African Americans make up just 9 percent of students in Advanced Placement classes nationally, as opposed to 15 percent of students overall. At the same time, Blacks make up a disproportionately large share of students assigned to remedial classes.

the college level as well. There is evidence, for example, that professors of all races pay less attention to Black students than to White students. In one experiment, researchers wrote to graduate school professors, posing as prospective students and expressing interest in the professors' field of study. Some of the letters were signed with names typical of White people, such as "Brad Anderson"; other names, such as "Keisha Thomas," were more commonly associated with Blacks. Overall, professors were much more likely to respond to these letters if they were signed by students with White-sounding names. These results certainly point to systemic racism in academia.

Other experts agree. In subtle ways, colleges discourage Black students from celebrating and reflecting their own cultures and push them into behaving more like White students. As psychology professor Claude M. Steele argues, these schools offer a difficult bargain to Black students. In order to be valued by the college, Steele writes, "[Black students] must give up many particulars of being black—styles of speech and appearance, value priorities, preferences—at least in mainstream settings."[43] The expectation that Blacks must change their behaviors in order to succeed in college is itself a form of racism.

At the same time, Black college students often are stereotyped in damaging ways by their professors and their fellow students. In one study, researcher Ebony O. McGee found that Black university students were often seen as less intelligent than White and Asian students. White students frequently assume that most of their Black classmates are in college as a result of affirmative action programs—that is, selected over more qualified White students in order to make the college a more racially diverse place. Other research suggests that professors are quick to dissuade Black students from taking courses viewed as especially hard. All are examples of institutional racism, which ultimately makes Black students feel that they do not belong in higher education.

Reducing Racism

The path to reduce systemic racism in America's schools seems particularly difficult. Educators and policy makers have known for years about the segregation of schools and the low funding for those with a Black majority. Some have sharply criticized the situation. As long ago as 1991, author Jonathan Kozol's book *Savage Inequalities* dealt with funding issues, especially for Black-majority schools, and concluded that low-income, heavily Black schools should get more money than White suburban schools, not less. The book was a best seller, but it did little to change the way schools are funded. Though Kozol and others have tried, they have made little headway against either segregation or unequal funding. And as long as White parents are uncomfortable sending their children to schools with large numbers of students of color, this will likely remain the case.

Nonetheless, education itself seems to be the best way forward for those who want to eliminate systemic racism in American schools. Several works of fiction and nonfiction lately have attempted to describe the institutional racism faced by Blacks at all levels of education. A television series called *Dear White People*, for example, tells of the racism experienced by Black students at a largely White college. Those who watch the series will certainly gain an appreciation of systemic racism as it manifests itself at the college level—and may be moved to do something about it.

Whether in kindergarten or in college, systemic racism is all too common within the US educational system. Black students are segregated from Whites, given fewer resources, punished more severely, and denied the opportunity to expand their education by taking more challenging courses. These examples of racism are bad enough in and of themselves, but they are made far worse because of the importance of education in today's society. Black students in underfunded schools miss out on opportunities that are afforded to White students in other schools—which in turn harms them in the job market, limits their earning potential, and in other ways perpetuates the inequality of African Americans as a group. As Robert Bravo, superintendent of a California school district, puts it, "We need to do more to continue the essential work to acknowledge, identify, and eliminate systemic racism in our schools."[44]

> "We need to do more to continue the essential work to acknowledge, identify, and eliminate systemic racism in our schools."[44]
>
> —Robert Bravo, superintendent of a California school district

CHAPTER FOUR

Policing and Incarceration

In March 2020 the police in Louisville, Kentucky, began looking for two men whom they believed to be drug dealers. The investigation led three police officers to an apartment rented by a twenty-six-year-old Black woman named Breonna Taylor; police believed that one of the men was using Taylor's apartment to receive drugs. The officers obtained a no-knock search warrant, which allowed them to enter the apartment without announcing their presence, and broke down Taylor's door just after midnight on March 13. The officers were out of uniform, and according to some witnesses—including Taylor's boyfriend, Kenneth Walker, who was in the apartment at the time—they never identified themselves as police officers. Believing that the officers were intruders, Walker shot and wounded one of the men. The officers in turn fired dozens of shots into the apartment. At least five bullets hit Taylor, and she died at the scene.

The tragic killing of Breonna Taylor sparked enormous anger in Louisville and beyond. As many observers saw it, Taylor's death was entirely unnecessary. The connection between Taylor and the supposed drug dealers was tenuous at best. No drugs were found in Taylor's apartment, and Louisville's postmaster later said that no suspicious packages had been delivered to Taylor's address. Moreover, many people argued that the police officers should have chosen another time to carry out the search.

Indeed, police records indicate that the officers did not expect to encounter trouble at Taylor's address. In this view, uniformed officers should have come to the apartment during daylight hours. As Taylor's mother puts it, "There is NO reason Breonna should be dead at all."[45]

To many observers, however, the tragedy of Taylor's story went deeper. Taylor, a Black woman, had been shot and killed by three White police officers—and her death was not an isolated event. Rather, it was just one of many incidents during 2020 in which Blacks were killed or severely injured by police officers. In May, George Floyd died in Minneapolis when a police officer placed his knee on Floyd's neck, cutting off the supply of air to Floyd's lungs. Floyd's last words were, "Man, I can't breathe."[46] In June, Rayshard Brooks of Atlanta was shot and killed in a parking lot while running away from two police officers. In August, Wisconsin resident Jacob Blake was shot multiple times in the back while opening his car door during an altercation with police; though Blake survived, he was seriously injured. Taylor, Floyd, Brooks, and Blake were all African American, and many people believe that their race is what brought about their injury or death. "Their only crime," writes journalist Joshua Santos, "was being black."[47]

To numerous observers, including millions who are not themselves African American, the sheer number of incidents like these is appalling. There is a pattern in which Blacks are being killed by largely White police forces, and many people blame systemic racism. "If Breonna Taylor were white, [her death] would never have happened," writes author Jim Wallis. "Period."[48] Indeed, the law enforcement community has been accused of institutional racism in several significant ways—from the number of times Blacks are stopped for minor traffic infractions to the lengths of prison sentences given to Blacks as compared to Whites. In 2020, sparked by the deaths of people like Taylor and Floyd, protesters took to

The killing of Breonna Taylor by white police officers in Louisville, Kentucky, sparked widespread protests against the use of deadly force by law enforcement authorities.

the streets all over America, demonstrating against police brutality and calling for an end to a system of law enforcement that seems to value Blacks less than Whites. Nonetheless, institutional racism continues to be a feature of the American system of law enforcement.

Treatment by Police

Sadly, the killing of Black people by police officers is nothing new. In 2014, for example, a Black man named Michael Brown was shot and killed by a White police officer in a suburb of St. Louis. The same year, Tamir Rice, a twelve-year-old African American boy, was fatally shot by a White officer in Cleveland. In 2015 Walter Scott of South Carolina was pulled over because he was driving with a broken brake light. When Scott tried to run from a White police officer, the officer fired his gun and killed him. Eric Garner was choked to death by White officers in New York in 2014; a year later Baltimore resident Freddie Gray died under mysterious circumstances while in police custody. There has been a long history of Blacks, particularly men, dying at the hands of White police officers.

The problem goes beyond anecdotes and individual events. In fact, statistics show that Black deaths at the hands of police are alarmingly common. Nationwide, African Americans are more than twice as likely as Whites to be shot and killed by the police. In some states, the disparity is considerably worse. In Utah just 1 percent of the population is African American, yet Blacks made up 10 percent of deaths at the hands of police officers during the same time period. These figures suggest that Blacks are being victimized simply because of their race.

Most law enforcement agencies spell out when it is appropriate for their officers to use deadly force. Most often, police are justified in using these tactics only in very specific circumstances, such as when their own lives or the lives of others are in immediate danger. In many recent cases involving police killings of unarmed Black men, however, cell phone videos and other evidence suggest that the offenders did not pose an imminent threat to police or bystanders. Michael Brown had stolen a package of cigars from a convenience store, for example, and Freddie Gray had been arrested for illegal possession of a knife. Neither man was armed at the time of his altercation with law enforcement officials. This was true of others as well. "Jacob Blake didn't harm anyone or pose any threat to the police,"[49] points out Blake's attorney.

Other Issues

Moreover, there are telltale differences in how police seem to treat Blacks and Whites in tense situations, such as making an arrest or chasing a suspect. In September 2020 Jason Mesich of Minnesota shot and killed his wife, then shot two of his neighbors, and finally barricaded himself in his basement. When officers came to the scene, Mesich, who is White, was still firing his gun. In an effort to defuse the situation, the responding officers began a conversation with Mesich and eventually convinced him to surrender. "Why do the police decide that some threats must be extinguished, while other threats get defused?" asks comedian and political commentator Trevor Noah. "We know the answer. . . . To some people, Black skin is the most threatening weapon of all."[50]

Racism in the legal system is evident in other areas, too. One example involves traffic stops, in which drivers are pulled over for speeding, failure to signal a turn, or some other infraction. According to studies conducted by the Stanford Open Polic-

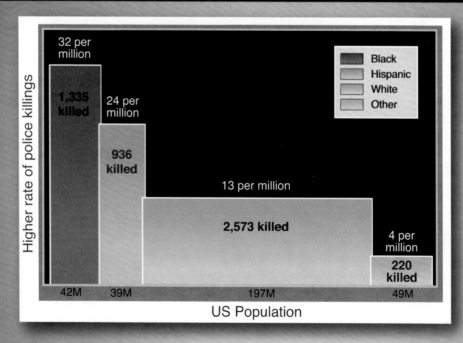

Black Americans Experience Higher Rate of Police Killings than White Americans

Police kill Black Americans at a much higher rate than White Americans, according to data collected by the *Washington Post* between 2015 and 2020. Actual numbers show that more Whites were killed by police during that period (2,573) than Blacks (1,335). But Blacks make up less than 13 percent of the US population compared with Whites, who make up 60 percent. Based on their numbers in the population, African Americans are being killed at a disproportionate rate of 32 per million versus 13 per million for Whites. The data also show a disproportionate rate of Hispanics killed by police.

Higher rate of police killings

Black
Hispanic
White
Other

32 per million
1,335 killed

24 per million
936 killed

13 per million
2,573 killed

4 per million
220 killed

42M   39M   197M   49M

US Population

Source: "Fatal Force," *Washington Post*, September 8, 2020.
https://www.washingtonpost.com/graphics/investigations/police-shootings-database/.

ing Project at Stanford University, Black drivers are much more likely than White drivers to be stopped for these reasons. That is especially true during daylight hours, when police can more easily discern a driver's race. Again, the conclusion is clear: at least some police officers do use race in deciding whether to pull a driver over. Indeed, some law enforcement officials acknowledge that discrimination does take place. "There are inequities in traffic stops," says Steve Linders, a spokesman for the St. Paul, Minnesota, police department. "It's fact."[51]

> **"There are inequities in traffic stops. It's fact."[51]**
>
> —Steve Linders, St. Paul, Minnesota, police spokesman

Searches, Interrogations, and Trials

Searches and interrogations are further examples of the way Blacks are singled out by law enforcement. One study revealed that 63 percent of the people searched or interrogated by Boston police are Black, even though African Americans make up just 24 percent of the city's population. "It's not that Black people are criminals," writes journalist Michael Harriot. "It's that the cops *think Black people are criminals*."[52]

Another example of systemic racism involves what happens when people go on trial. Blacks are more likely than Whites to be convicted of certain crimes, especially those involving drugs and weapons. A Harvard Law School study of Massachusetts revealed that in 2012, just 16 percent of the people charged with gun offenses were African American, but Blacks accounted for 46 percent of the convictions. The same study found that Blacks are also typically given longer prison sentences than Whites even when they commit the same crimes.

The death penalty, too, is applied unequally. As the National Association for the Advancement of Colored People (NAACP) points out, "African Americans are pursued, convicted, and sent to death at a disproportionately higher rate than any other race."[53] Though Blacks make up about 13 percent of the population, they account for about 35 percent of executions. And African Americans are especially likely to be given a death sentence if they have killed a White person. Over a period of several years in Georgia, 22 percent of Blacks who were convicted of killing White people received the death penalty, compared to just 1 percent of Blacks who killed other Blacks and 3 percent of Whites who killed African Americans. This is another example of institutional racism in the court system. As many legal experts note, neither the race of the victim nor the race of the perpetrator should affect the severity of the sentence—and yet it does.

The result of these disparities is not surprising. With so many Blacks being searched, convicted, and given long sentences, African Americans make up an enormous share of the prison population in the United States. About 34 percent of prison inmates are Black—which is two to three times greater than their share of the general population. The average Black man is about five times more likely to be incarcerated than the average White man. Roughly one African American man out of every six is in jail or prison at any given time. And hundreds of thousands of those who are free were incarcerated at some point in their lives. Legal scholar and author Michelle Alexander estimates that three-fourths of young African American men today will spend at least some time in prison during their lives.

The high incarceration rates have an enormous effect on prisoners and their families—and on society at large. Being in prison often means the loss of civil rights such as voting—indeed, in many states felons cannot vote even after they are released. Incarceration damages inmates' health, too, and often leads to premature death. When people are imprisoned, their families suffer economic hardship and mental distress. Their children are more likely to be expelled from school and much more likely to become

Trayvon Martin and Black Lives Matter

In 2012 an unarmed seventeen-year-old African American high school student named Trayvon Martin was confronted by a man named George Zimmerman while walking near his Florida home. Zimmerman thought that Martin was planning a crime. During an ensuing struggle, Zimmerman shot Martin to death. Many people, both Black and White, urged that Zimmerman be arrested and charged with murder. But police investigators determined that Zimmerman had acted in self-defense—a decision that appalled much of the nation.

The Martin case was just one event in a long line of killings of Blacks by police and others, and the fact that Zimmerman was not convicted of murder made it seem particularly bad. In 2013 three Black women—Alicia Garza, Patrisse Cullors, and Opal Tometi—founded an organization they called Black Lives Matter. The organization's purpose was to fight back against police brutality, protest the killings of people like Trayvon Martin, and more generally to attack White supremacy while upholding the value of Black people. Today the organization is probably the best known of all the groups dedicated to fighting for Black people's rights.

involved in criminal activity themselves. Locking up so many people is extremely costly, too; together, the federal government and the states spend an estimated $80 billion a year on corrections. If Black people were incarcerated at the same rate as White people, a large chunk of this money would be saved.

Education, Protest, and Other Strategies

Antiracism activists often argue that education is key to meaningful change. The more information people have about systemic racism in law enforcement, the more likely they are to see it as a serious problem that needs to be fixed. One effective way of informing people is through the media. As with other aspects of systemic racism, there are plenty of books and films describing issues of race in policing and incarceration. A documentary called

In hundreds of demonstrations against police brutality during the spring and summer of 2020, marchers protested systemic racism in the nation's criminal justice system.

Rest in Power: The Trayvon Martin Case, for example, describes the events that led to the shooting of an unarmed Black teenager by a white vigilante in 2012, which sparked the formation of the advocacy group Black Lives Matter. Michelle Alexander's best-selling book *The New Jim Crow: Mass Incarceration in the Age of Colorblindness* argues that racism in policing and incarceration has turned Blacks, especially Black men, into second-class citizens. These works and others like them have helped raise awareness of systemic racism in America.

One strategy for increasing awareness is for celebrities to take up the cause. The events of late August 2020 are a good example. Three days after Jacob Blake was shot by police in Kenosha, Wisconsin, the Milwaukee Bucks of the National Basketball Association (NBA)—whose home arena is only a few dozen miles from Kenosha—decided not to play their scheduled playoff game against the Orlando Magic. The Bucks issued a statement explaining their actions. It read, in part:

When we take the court and represent Milwaukee and Wisconsin, we are expected to play at a high level, give maximum effort, and hold each other accountable. We hold ourselves to that standard, and in this moment, we are demanding the same from our lawmakers and law enforcement. We are calling for justice for Jacob Blake and demand the officers be held accountable.[54]

The Magic could have claimed victory by forfeit, but in solidarity with the Bucks, they too refused to play. The game was postponed. The Bucks' anger and resolve swiftly spread throughout the NBA and into other professional sports leagues as well. All

Penalties for Police Officers

One indicator of systemic racism in the world of law enforcement involves the treatment of the police officers who were responsible for killing Blacks. In general, law enforcement officials have been reluctant to do much to discipline these officers. The four officers involved in George Floyd's death were all fired from the Minneapolis police force the day following the incident, but more often police escape serious consequences. The officers responsible for the shooting of Tamir Rice did not lose their jobs. And while some police officers have been brought up on criminal charges, others have not—and few have been convicted. Of the three officers who killed Breonna Taylor, for instance, two escaped criminal charges of any kind, and the third was charged with a minor offense; none were tried for murder or manslaughter.

In some cases it has even seemed as if law enforcement officials are closing ranks around the killers. In the case of Tamir Rice, prosecutor Tim McGinty looked into charging Rice's killers with a crime but ultimately declined. Moreover, he hired expert witnesses to help demonstrate to a grand jury that the officers were innocent—an action that particularly infuriated Rice's mother. "Prosecutor McGinty deliberately sabotaged the case," she asserts, "never advocating for my son, and acting instead like the police officers' defense attorney."

Quoted in Emily Shapiro, "Tamir Rice Case: Prosecutor Abused, Manipulated Grand Jury Process, Family Attorneys Say," ABC News, December 28, 2015. https://abcnews.go.com.

NBA playoff games were canceled for several days. The National Hockey League and the Women's National Basketball Association paused their seasons as well. In addition, more than a dozen Major League Baseball games were postponed due to mutual agreement between the teams; some players draped Black Lives Matter banners across home plate to show their support for change. "At some point, actions speak louder than words,"[55] says Milwaukee Brewers outfielder Ryan Braun. Sports fans everywhere took note.

Organized protests can be effective as well. During the spring and summer of 2020, there were hundreds of demonstrations against police brutality, many led by Black Lives Matter. Most of these were held in well-traveled public areas, such as the area near the White House in Washington, DC, and other places where protesters would be highly visible. People taking part in these demonstrations chanted, sang, displayed signs, and in other ways showed their dedication to their cause. Though the value of protests can be difficult to measure, there is some evidence that demonstrations like these can achieve their goals. "Protests change minds and shift public opinion,"[56] writes journalist Rosemary Westwood. Certainly, these protests had an effect: surveys taken during the summer of 2020 revealed that a majority of Americans supported the protesters and their goals.

Race matters within the law enforcement system. A Black person is far more likely than a White person to be stopped by police or put in prison and is far more likely than a White person to be killed by the police or by the state. Even when offenses are identical, the penalty is often greater for an African American than for a White person. The main reason for this situation is systemic racism. The United States has constructed a system of law enforcement in which the races are treated unequally. As law professor Khiara M. Bridges writes, "The criminal-justice system evidences the way a society that should care for and protect its people instead leaves black people susceptible to harm and with little control over their well-being."[57] Any reform of the criminal justice system must begin with an end to systemic racism.

Introduction: The Roots of Systemic Racism

1. Quoted in Meghan E. Irons, "Researchers Expected 'Outrageously High' Discrimination Against Black Renters. What They Found Was Worse than Imagined," *Boston Globe*, July 1, 2020. www.bostonglobe.com.

2. Shayanne Gal et al., "26 Simple Charts to Show Friends and Family Who Aren't Convinced Racism Is Still a Problem in America," Business Insider, July 8, 2020. www.business insider.com.

3. Quoted in Halimah Abdullah, "What Do Terms like Systemic Racism, Microaggression and White Fragility Actually Mean?," ABC News, June 14, 2020. https://abcnews .go.com.

Chapter One: Health

4. Kristen Jordan Shamus, "Family Ravaged by Coronavirus Begged for Tests, Hospital Care but Was Repeatedly Denied," *USA Today*, April 20, 2020. www.usatoday.com.

5. Quoted in Shamus, "Family Ravaged by Coronavirus Begged for Tests, Hospital Care but Was Repeatedly Denied."

6. Quoted in Shamus, "Family Ravaged by Coronavirus Begged for Tests, Hospital Care but Was Repeatedly Denied."

7. Quoted in Maria Godoy and Daniel Wood, "What Do Coronavirus Racial Disparities Look like State by State?," NPR, May 30, 2020. www.npr.org.

8. Quoted in Carolyn Y. Johnson, "Racial Inequality Even Affects How Long We Wait for the Doctor," *Washington Post*, October 5, 2015. www.washingtonpost.com.

9. Robert Pearl, "Why Health Care Is Different If You're Black, Latino, or Poor," *Forbes*, March 5, 2015. www.forbes.com.

10. Yolonda Wilson, "Dying While Black," The Conversation, February 5, 2019. https://theconversation.com.

11. Quoted in Valeria Escobar, "Segregation Exposes Black Residents to Health Risks. Hospitals Are Disincentivized from Treating Them," *Columbia Daily Spectator*, April 18, 2020. www.columbiaspectator.com.

12. Quoted in Sujata Gupta, "Why African-Americans May Be Especially Vulnerable to COVID-19," *Science News*, April 10, 2020. www.sciencenews.org.

13. Quoted in Shamus, "Family Ravaged by Coronavirus Begged for Tests, Hospital Care but Was Repeatedly Denied."

14. Quoted in John J. Miller, "John James, the Michigan GOP's Rising Star," *National Review*, June 1, 2020. www.national review.com.

15. Joseph V. Sakran et al., "Racism in Health Care Isn't Always Obvious," *Scientific American*, July 9, 2020. www.scientific american.com.

Chapter Two: Employment

16. Dave Zirin, "Why Are There So Few Black Coaches in the NFL? It's the Racism, Stupid," *The Nation*, January 10, 2020. www.thenation.com.

17. Quoted in Dave Fymbo, "Black Coaches Matter: Systemic Racism in the NFL," Medium, June 8, 2020. https://medium .com.

18. Fymbo, "Black Coaches Matter."

19. Gal et al., "26 Simple Charts to Show Friends and Family Who Aren't Convinced Racism Is Still a Problem in America."

20. Quoted in Khristopher J. Brooks, "Why So Many Black Business Professionals Are Missing from the C-Suite," CBS News, December 10, 2019. www.cbsnews.com.

21. Quoted in Anne Neborak, "A Beautiful Outlook for Job Seekers," Delaware County News Network, November 15, 2016. www.delconewsnetwork.com.

22. Quoted in Susan Adams, "Networking Is Still the Best Way to Find a Job, Survey Says," *Forbes*, June 7, 2011. www.forbes.com.
23. Ruqaiijah Yearby, "The Impact of Structural Racism in Employment and Wages on Minority Women's Health," American Bar Association. www.americanbar.org.
24. Quoted in Neil Shah, "Need for Networking Puts Black Job Seekers at a Disadvantage," *Wall Street Journal*, March 27, 2017. https://blogs.wsj.com.
25. Elise Gould, "Black-White Wage Gaps Are Worse Today than in 2000," Economics Policy Institute, February 27, 2020. www.epi.org.
26. Quoted in Karen Yuan, "Working While Black: Stories from Black Corporate America," *Fortune*, June 16, 2020. https://fortune.com.
27. Quoted in Gene Demby, "Racial Disparities in Wages Boil Down to Discrimination," NPR, September 23, 2016. www.npr.org.
28. Shahar Ziv, "Salary History Bans Reduce Racial and Gender Wage Gaps; Every CEO Should Use Them," *Forbes*, June 23, 2020. www.forbes.com.
29. Ziv, "Salary History Bans Reduce Racial and Gender Wage Gaps; Every CEO Should Use Them."
30. Levy Vinick Burrell Hyams, "What Can You Do to Combat Systemic Racism at Work in California?," 2020. https://levyvinick.com.
31. Jayne Thompson, "How to Prevent Racism in the Workplace," Small Business Chronicle, January 24, 2019. https://smallbusiness.chron.com.

Chapter Three: Education

32. Quoted in Annie Waldman et al., "Charlottesville's Other Jim Crow Legacy: Separate and Unequal Education," ProPublica, October 16, 2018. www.propublica.org.
33. Quoted in Bill Hand, "Kinston Students Were Pioneers in Civil Rights," *New Bern (NC) Sun Journal*, August 4, 2019. www.newbernsj.com.

34. Quoted in Brian Duignan, "Brown v. Board of Education of Topeka," *Encyclopaedia Britannica Online*, 2020. www.britannica.com.

35. Clare Lombardo, "Why White School Districts Have So Much More Money," NPR, February 26, 2019. www.npr.org.

36. Quoted in Matt Barnum, "4 New Studies Bolster the Case: More Money for Schools Helps Low-Income Students," Chalkbeat, August 13, 2019. www.chalkbeat.org.

37. Alana Semuels, "Good School, Rich School; Bad School, Poor School," *The Atlantic*, August 2016. www.theatlantic.com.

38. Quoted in Lauren Camera, "Segregation Reinforced by School Districts," *U.S. News & World Report*, July 25, 2019. www.usnews.com.

39. Alvin Chang, "White America Is Quietly Self-Segregating," Vox, January 18, 2017. www.vox.com.

40. Quoted in Laura Faith Kebede and Caroline Bauman, "A 'Told You So' About Breakaway School Districts Leaves Out Urban District Left Behind," Chalkbeat, August 4, 2017. https://tn.chalkbeat.org.

41. Quoted in German Lopez, "Black Kids Are Way More Likely to Be Punished in School than White Kids, Study Finds," Vox, April 5, 2018. www.vox.com.

42. Quoted in Matt Barnum, "Racially Integrated High Schools Often Conceal Segregated Classes, New Study Shows," Chalkbeat, March 4, 2020. www.chalkbeat.org.

43. Quoted in Adrienne Green, "The Cost of Balancing Academia and Racism," *The Atlantic*, January 2016. www.theatlantic.com.

44. Quoted in Campbell Union High School District, "CUHSD Board of Trustees Approve Resolution Denouncing Racism, White Supremacy and Declaring #BlackLivesMatter." www.cuhsd.org.

Chapter Four: Policing and Incarceration

45. Quoted in Anna North and Fabiola Cineas, "Breanna Taylor Was Killed by Police in March. The Officers Involved Have Not Been Arrested," Vox, May 13, 2020. www.vox.com.

46. Quoted in Joshua Rhett Miller, "Police Footage Shows George Floyd's Last Words: 'Man, I Can't Breathe,'" *New York Post*, July 15, 2020. https://nypost.com.

47. Joshua Santos, "We Must Stand Up for Black People," *Cornwall (ON) Standard-Freeholder*, June 2, 2020. www.standard-freeholder.com.

48. Jim Wallis, "If Breonna Taylor Were White," Twitter, May 14, 2020, 12:56 p.m. https://twitter.com/jimwallis/status/1260977399967211529.

49. Quoted in Katie DeLong, "'Jacob Blake Didn't Pose Any Threat,'" Fox6 Milwaukee, August 27, 2020. www.fox6now.com.

50. Quoted in *Haaretz* (Tel Aviv, Israel), "Trevor Noah: Why Was Jacob Blake Shot 7 Times but Kyle Rittenhouse Wasn't a Threat," August 27, 2020. www.haaretz.com.

51. Quoted in Erik Ortiz, "Inside 100 Million Police Traffic Stops: New Evidence of Racial Bias," NBC News, March 13, 2019. www.nbcnews.com.

52. Michael Harriot, "A Judge Asked Harvard to Find Out Why So Many Black People Were in Prison," The Root, September 10, 2020. www.theroot.com.

53. National Association for the Advancement of Colored People, "Criminal Justice Fact Sheet," 2020. www.naacp.org.

54. Quoted in Nick Greene, "The Milwaukee Bucks Players' Strike Instantly Seems Like It Was Inevitable," Slate, August 26, 2020. https://slate.com.

55. Quoted in Dayn Perry, "Milwaukee Brewers Join Bucks in Protest, Sit Out Game vs. Reds After Jacob Blake Shooting," CBS Sports, August 27, 2020. www.cbssports.com.

56. Rosemary Westwood, "Protests Change Minds and Shift Public Opinion. That's Why Opponents Are Quick to Disparage Them," CBC News, March 6, 2017. www.cbc.ca.

57. Khiara M. Bridges, "The Many Ways Institutional Racism Kills Black People," *Time*, June 11, 2020. https://time.com.

ORGANIZATIONS AND WEBSITES

American Civil Liberties Union
www.aclu.org

This organization has been fighting for civil rights for more than a century. The civil rights of Black people are among the group's primary interests. The site offers information about the group's policies, offers ways for people to get involved in the ACLU's activities, and updates of news items important to the organization.

Black Lives Matter
www.blacklivesmatter.org

Founded by three Black women in 2013, this is the most famous organization focused on battling White supremacy and racism and pushing back against police brutality toward African Americans. The site provides links to news items, information on the history of White supremacy and police brutality, and statements from the organization about current events.

Color of Change
www.colorofchange.org

This organization fights against injustice toward Black Americans, including issues of voting, health, economics, and White supremacy. Its website includes links to various campaigns designed to attack and end racism around the world.

National Association for the Advancement of Colored People (NAACP)
www.naacp.org

The NAACP was established in 1909 to defend the rights of Blacks and push for greater participation in society for African

Americans. It continues to battle racism and work for Black people everywhere. Its website provides volunteer opportunities as well as fact sheets and other information about race.

National Museum of African American History & Culture
www.nmaahc.si.edu

This museum is part of the Smithsonian Institution. It provides a historical perspective on Black culture and offers antiracism educational materials, such as information about how to talk with other people about race. Its website also includes links to the museum's collections and exhibits.

Teaching Tolerance
www.tolerance.org

This is primarily an educational organization. Its main focus is on providing classroom resources to help students adopt an antiracist perspective. Its website offers classroom resources, professional development materials, and many articles and other publications dealing with race and racism.

Books

Michelle Alexander, *The New Jim Crow*. Tenth Anniversary Edition. New York: New Press, 2020.

Tehama Lopez Bunyasi and Candis Watts Smith, eds., *Stay Woke: A People's Guide to Making All Black Lives Matter*. New York: New York University, 2019.

Ibram X. Kendi, *How to Be an Antiracist*. New York: Penguin, 2019.

Ibram X. Kendi, *Stamped from the Beginning: The Definitive History of Racist Ideas in America*. New York: Hachette, 2017.

Hal Marcovitz, *Black in America*. San Diego, CA: ReferencePoint, 2021.

Alex Zamalin, *Antiracism*. New York: New York University, 2019.

Internet Sources

Halimah Abdullah, "What Do Terms like Systemic Racism, Microaggression and White Fragility Actually Mean?," ABC News, June 14, 2020. https://abcnews.go.com.

Khiara M. Bridges, "The Many Ways Institutional Racism Kills Black People," *Time*, June 11, 2020. https://time.com.

Lauren Camera, "Segregation Reinforced by School Districts," *U.S. News & World Report*, July 25, 2019. www.usnews.com.

Shayanne Gal et al., "26 Simple Charts to Show Friends and Family Who Aren't Convinced Racism Is Still a Problem in America," Business Insider, July 8, 2020. www.businessinsider.com.

Erik Ortiz, "Inside 100 Million Police Traffic Stops: New Evidence of Racial Bias," NBC News, March 13, 2019. www.nbcnews.com.

Robert Pearl, "Why Health Care Is Different If You're Black, Latino, or Poor," *Forbes*, March 5, 2015. www.forbes.com.

Joseph V. Sakran et al., "Racism in Health Care Isn't Always Obvious," *Scientific American*, July 9, 2020. www.scientificamerican.com.

Annie Waldman et al., "Charlottesville's Other Jim Crow Legacy: Separate and Unequal Education," ProPublica, October 16, 2018. www.propublica.org.

Karen Yuan, "Working While Black: Stories from Black Corporate America," *Fortune*, June 16, 2020. https://fortune.com.

Note: Boldface page numbers indicate illustrations.

Alexander, Michelle, 48, 50
algorithms and race, 15
American Bar Association, 25
Anto-Ocrah, Martina, 14
Atlanta, Georgia, 43

Baltimore, Maryland, 44–45
Berman, William, 5
Black Lives Matter, 49, **50**, 52
Blake, Jacob, 43, 45, 50
Bloomberg, Michael, 35
Boston, Massachusetts, housing
    discrimination in, 4–5, **6**
Braun, Ryan, 52
Bravo, Robert, 41
breast cancer
    deaths, 9, **12**
    preventive care and treatment of, 11,
        12
Brewer, Rosalind, 24
Bridgeport, Connecticut, 34
Bridges, Khiara M., 52
Brooks, Rayshard, 43
Brown, Michael, 44, 45
Brown v. Board of Education (1954), 31
Bureau of Labor Statistics, 20
Business Insider (website), 5, 21

California, 18
cancer and race, 9
car availability and race, 17
Centers for Disease Control and
    Prevention (CDC), 9
Chang, Alvin, 37
Charlottesville, Virginia, 30, 35
Chenault, Kenneth, 21–22
Chicago, Illinois, 36
childcare programs and race, 33
Cleveland, Ohio, 44
colleges and universities, 38–40
computers and race
    algorithms used in health care, 15

internet and job openings, 22–23, **23**
coronavirus, 8–10, **10**
court system and race, 47–49
COVID-19 and race
    employment and, 28
    infection rates, 14
    testing, 17
    treatment of and deaths from, 8–10,
        10
Coward, Charles, 31
Cullors, Patrisse, 49

Day, Caitlin, 22
Dear White People (television program),
    41
death penalty and race, 47–48
death rates and race, 9, **12**
Detroit, Michigan, 8, 18
diabetes, 9, 11
DiTomaso, Nancy, 25

early childhood education and race, 33
earnings and race. *See* income and race
education and race
    advanced courses, 30, 38, **39**
    Black children viewed as older than
        actual age and, 38
    colleges and universities, 38–40
    current segregation of schools, 31
        funding and, 32–34
        geography as cause of, 35–37
        shifting of school boundaries and, 37
    funding, 31, 32–34
    gifted and talented programs, 30, 38
    income and, 36–37
    legal segregation of schools, 31, **34**
    measures to end systemic racism,
        40–41
    preschool, 33
    reading levels, 30
    remedial classes, 38
    standardized tests, 36
    stereotypes and, 40
    suspensions and expulsions, 30, 33,
        37–38, 48

wage disparity and education level, 26–27
employment and race
  Black executives and mentoring, 24
  COVID-19 and, 14, 28
  hiring and firing, 20, 29
  internet and job openings, 22–23, **23**
  measures to end systemic racism, 27–29
  networking, 23–25
  NFL players and management, 19–20
  pay, 20
  in professional fields, 21–22
  rates of unemployment, 20–21
  recruiting and hiring, **27**
  stereotypes and, 25–26
end of life care, 12

Fangio, Vic, 19
Florida, 49
Floyd, George, 43, 51
Forbes (magazine), 23
Fowler family, 8–9
Fymbo, Dave, 20

Gambrell, Keith, 8–9, 10
Garner, Eric, 44
Garza, Alicia, 49
Georgia, 48
Goff, Phillip, 38
Gould, Elise, 26
Gray, Freddie, 44–45
Green, Alexander, 11, 12–13
Greenhouse, Steven, 28
Grier, Chris, 19, **21**

Harriot, Michael, 47
Head Start, 33
health and race
  complaints of pain, 11–12
  computer algorithms and, 15
  diagnosis and preventive care, 11
  diseases and conditions more common among Blacks than Whites, 9
  end of life care, 12
  hospital emergency room care, 8–9, 10, 11
  insurance, 13–14, 15
  measures to end systemic racism, 16–18
  medical treatment received, 11, 12–13, 15
  treatment of higher-status African Americans, 15

See also COVID-19 and race
high blood pressure, 18
Hispanics, deaths at hands of police, **46**
history of racism, 5–7
housing and race
  discrimination study of (2020), 4–5, **6**
  education and, 36–37
  low-income complexes, 14
  school segregation and, 35
Hughes, Trinity, 30

incarceration and race, 47–49
income and race
  disparity between Blacks and Whites, 13, 26–27
  education and, 36–37
  funding schools and, 32–34
  housing and, 14
  salary histories and, 27–28
institutional racism. *See* systemic racism

Jackson, Kirabo, 33
James, John, 17
Jim Crow laws, 6, 7
Johnson-Staub, Christine, 33
Journal of American Medicine, 12
judicial system and race, 47–49

Kenosha, Wisconsin, 43, 45, 50
Khaldun, Joneigh, 15
Kozol, Jonathan, 40

LaVeist, Thomas, 14
law enforcement and race. *See* policing and race
life expectancy and race, 9
Linders, Steve, 47
Lombardo, Clare, 32
Louisville, Kentucky, 42–43

Major League Baseball games, 52
Martin, Trayvon, 49
McGee, Ebony O., 40
McGinty, Tim, 51
"Medicare for all" health insurance system, 16–17
Mesich, Jason, 45–46
Miami Dolphins, 19, **21**
Milwaukee Bucks (NBA), 50–51
Minneapolis, Minnesota, 43, 51

National Association for the Advancement of Colored People (NAACP), 47

National Basketball Association (NBA), 50–52
National Football League (NFL), 19–20, **21**
National Hockey League, 52
Neal, Mark Anthony, 7
The New Jim Crow: Mass Incarceration in the Age of Colorblindness (Alexander), 50
New London, Connecticut, 34
New York City, 44
Noah, Trevor, 46
Nunez-Smith, Marcella, 9, 10

Patrick, Kayla, 38
Pearl, Robert, 11
peer-to-peer education, 18
Pew Research Center, 22
Philadelphia, Pennsylvania, 36
policing and race
  crime of "being Black," 42–43
  deaths at hands of police, 45, **46**
  defusing situations and, 45–46
  measures to end systemic racism in, 49–52
  protests sparked by killings of Blacks, 43–44
  searches and interrogations, 47
  traffic stops, 43, 44, 46–47
  treatment of officers responsible for killing Blacks, 51
Poughkeepsie, New York, 35
power, holders of, 7
preschool education and race, 33
prison population and race, 48–49

Rest in Power: The Trayvon Martin Case (documentary), 50
Rice, Tamir, 44, 51

safety net hospitals, 14
Sam's Club, 24
Sanders, Bernie, 16
Santos, Joshua, 43
Savage Inequalities (Kozol), 40
Sawyer, Tami, 37
Scarsdale, New York, 33
Scientific American (magazine), 17–18
Scott, Walter, 44
segregation
  in education, 31–37, **34**
  Jim Crow laws and, 6, 7
Semuels, Alana, 34
Shelby County, Tennessee, 37
slavery, 5
smartphone ownership and race, 22
Smith, Maya, 28
St. Louis, Missouri, 44
Stanford Open Policing Project, 46–47
Steele, Claude M., 39–40
Suffolk University Law School, 4–5
Suggs, Jennifer, 28
systemic racism
  described, 5
  in housing, 4–5, **6**
  measures to end in
    education, 40–41
    employment, 27–29
    health care, 16–18
    policing, 49–52
  NFL example of, 19–20, **21**
  White people as holders of power and, 7

Taylor, Breonna, 42–44, **44**, 51
Tometi, Opal, 49
transportation and race, **16**, 17

unconscious bias, 7
unemployment and race, 20–21
universities, 38–40
University of Pennsylvania, 11
US Supreme Court, 31
Utah, 45

Wake County, North Carolina, 36
Walker, Kenneth, 42
Wallis, Jim, 43
Warren, Earl, 31
wealth and race, 13
Westwood, Rosemary, 52
White people, power and unconscious bias of, 7
Wilson, Yolonda, 12
Women's National Basketball Association, 52

Zimmerman, George, 49
Zirin, Dave, 19
Ziv, Shahar, 27–28

DIGGING UP THE PAST

POMPEII

BY EMILY ROSE OACHS

BELLWETHER MEDIA • MINNEAPOLIS, MN

TM

Are you ready to take it to the extreme? Torque books thrust you into the action-packed world of sports, vehicles, mystery, and adventure. These books may include dirt, smoke, fire, and chilling tales. **WARNING**: read at your own risk.

This edition first published in 2020 by Bellwether Media, Inc.

No part of this publication may be reproduced in whole or in part without written permission of the publisher. For information regarding permission, write to Bellwether Media, Inc., Attention: Permissions Department, 6012 Blue Circle Drive, Minnetonka, MN 55343.

Library of Congress Cataloging-in-Publication Data

Names: Oachs, Emily Rose, author.
Title: Pompeii / By Emily Rose Oachs.
Description: Minneapolis, MN : Bellwether Media, Inc., 2020. | Series:
    Torque: Digging Up the Past | Includes bibliographical references and
    index. | Audience: Grades 3-7.
Identifiers: LCCN 2018061017 (print) | LCCN 2019001668 (ebook) |
    ISBN 9781618916419 (ebook) | ISBN 9781644870693 (hardcover :
    alk. paper)
Subjects: LCSH: Pompeii (Extinct city)–Juvenile literature. | Vesuvius
    (Italy)–Eruption, 79–Juvenile literature.
Classification: LCC DG70.P7 (ebook) | LCC DG70.P7 O23 2020 (print)
    | DDC 937/.7256807–dc23
LC record available at https://lccn.loc.gov/2018061017

Editor: Betsy Rathburn   Designer: Brittany McIntosh

Printed in the United States of America, North Mankato, MN.

TABLE OF CONTENTS

A CITY FROZEN IN TIME   4

WHAT IS POMPEII?   6

DISCOVERED IN THE ASH   12

STEPPING BACK IN TIME   18

GLOSSARY   22

TO LEARN MORE   23

INDEX   24

A CITY FROZEN IN TIME

Walking through a tall arch, you enter an **ancient** city. A large stone wall surrounds the city. Many nearby buildings are now **ruins**.

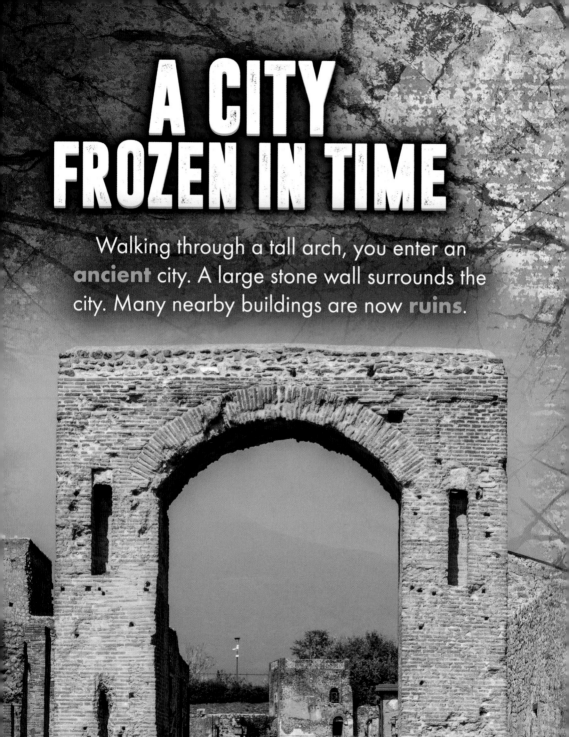

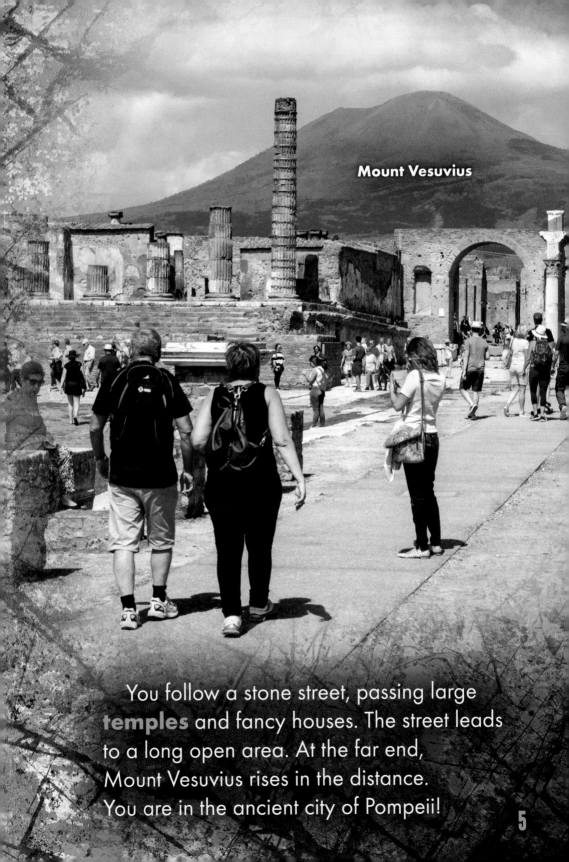

Mount Vesuvius

You follow a stone street, passing large **temples** and fancy houses. The street leads to a long open area. At the far end, Mount Vesuvius rises in the distance. You are in the ancient city of Pompeii!

WHAT IS POMPEII?

Pompeii was a city in the **Roman Empire**. Today, it is in modern Italy. It sat about 6 miles (10 kilometers) from the **volcano** Mount Vesuvius.

WHERE IS POMPEII?

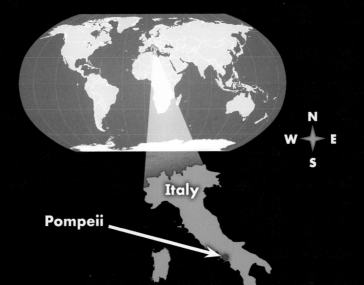

Italy

Pompeii

People first settled in Pompeii nearly 2,000 years ago. The city became a busy port on what is now the Sarno River. As many as 20,000 people lived there. It was also a popular vacation spot.

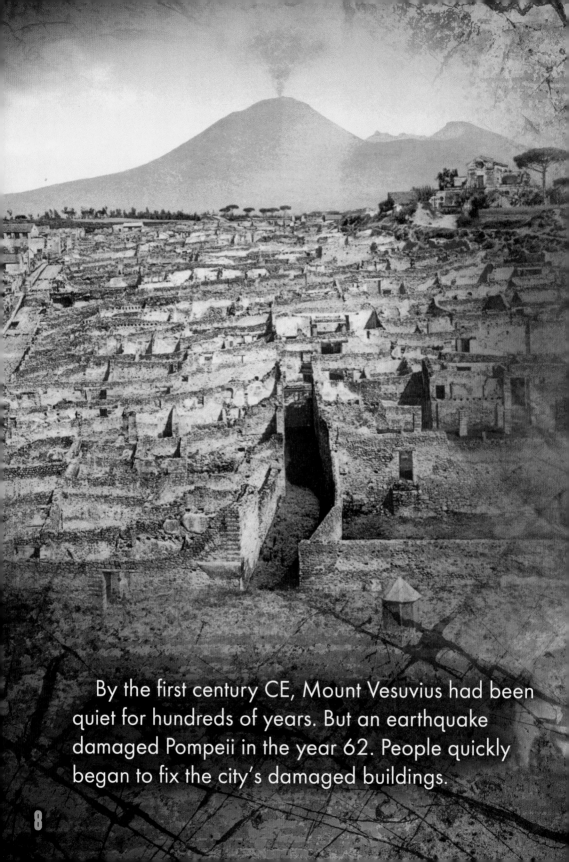

By the first century CE, Mount Vesuvius had been quiet for hundreds of years. But an earthquake damaged Pompeii in the year 62. People quickly began to fix the city's damaged buildings.

It would all be for nothing. In the year 79, Mount Vesuvius exploded into life!

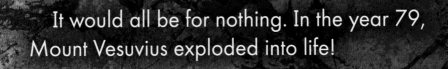

FAMOUS WITNESS

An author named Pliny the Younger saw the eruption from across the Bay of Naples. He described the huge cloud that rose from the volcano. He compared it to a tree!

POMPEII TIMELINE

700s BCE:
People begin settling the area
that will become Pompeii

79 CE:
Mount Vesuvius erupts, burying Pompeii
with ash and killing thousands of people

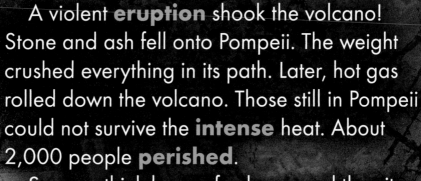

A violent **eruption** shook the volcano! Stone and ash fell onto Pompeii. The weight crushed everything in its path. Later, hot gas rolled down the volcano. Those still in Pompeii could not survive the **intense** heat. About 2,000 people **perished**.

Soon, a thick layer of ash covered the city. Pompeii disappeared for 1,700 years.

LOST CITIES

Pompeii was not the only city lost to Mount Vesuvius. The nearby cities of Herculaneum and Stabiae were also destroyed.

1748:
Charles III, King of Naples, sends workers to begin digging up Pompeii

2012:
The Great Pompeii Project forms to protect and restore Pompeii

1590s:
Domenico Fontana discovers the remains of Pompeii

1863:
Giuseppe Fiorelli takes charge of the Pompeii excavations, using plaster to make casts of victims' bodies

11

DISCOVERED IN THE ASH

In the 1590s, Domenico Fontana was digging a tunnel near Mount Vesuvius. While digging, he came across Pompeii's remains. Yet no **excavation** began there until 1748.

excavation

During the excavation, experts unearthed a city frozen in time. The ash had destroyed Pompeii. But it also **preserved** the city. Parts of Pompeii stood as they had in the year 79.

13

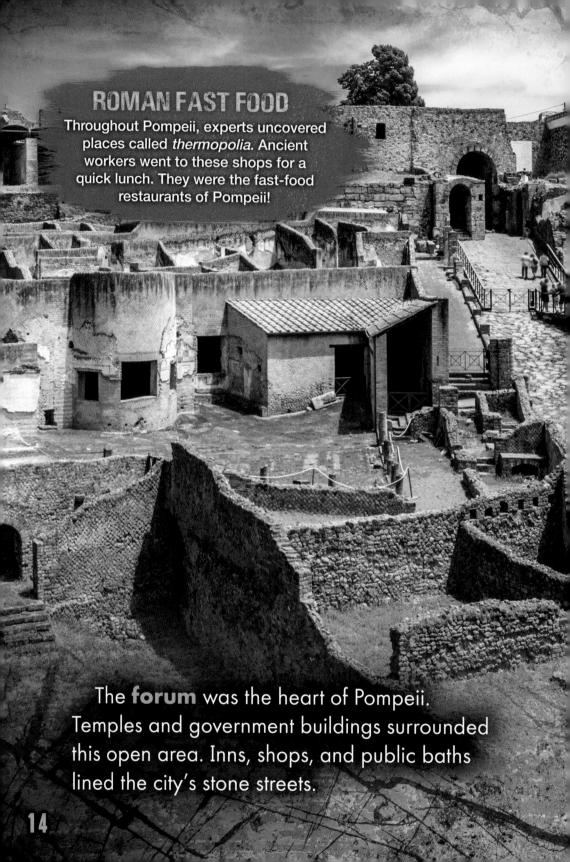

ROMAN FAST FOOD

Throughout Pompeii, experts uncovered places called *thermopolia*. Ancient workers went to these shops for a quick lunch. They were the fast-food restaurants of Pompeii!

The **forum** was the heart of Pompeii. Temples and government buildings surrounded this open area. Inns, shops, and public baths lined the city's stone streets.

Some of Pompeii's homes were small and simple. Others were grand houses. These homes showed what life was like for the rich and poor of Pompeii.

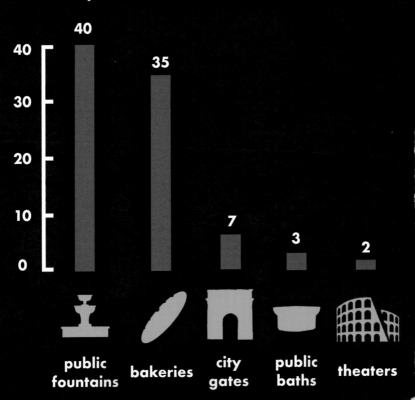

RUINS OF POMPEII

How many of each ruin have been found in Pompeii?

public fountains	40
bakeries	35
city gates	7
public baths	3
theaters	2

fresco

mosaic

Inside buildings, beautiful **fresco** paintings still decorated the walls. They showed scenes of the gods and everyday life. **Mosaics** also patterned the floors.

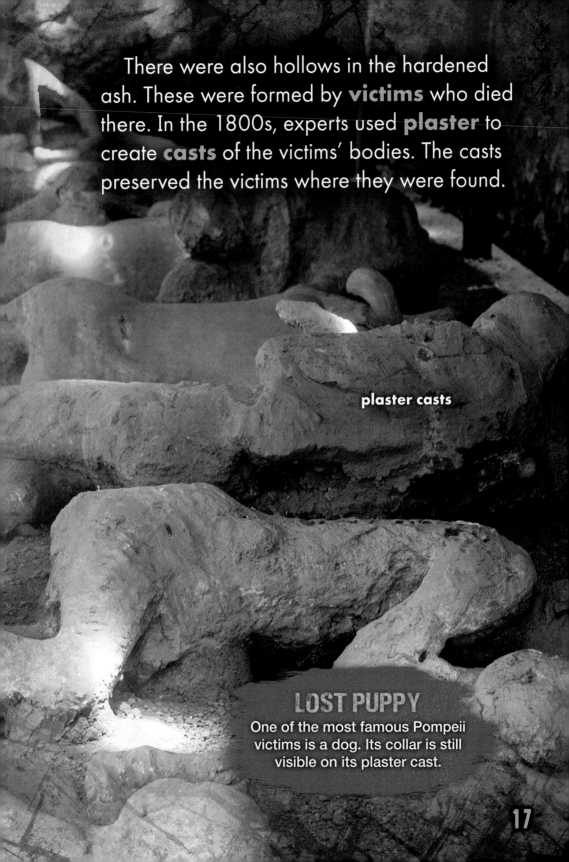

There were also hollows in the hardened ash. These were formed by **victims** who died there. In the 1800s, experts used **plaster** to create **casts** of the victims' bodies. The casts preserved the victims where they were found.

plaster casts

LOST PUPPY
One of the most famous Pompeii victims is a dog. Its collar is still visible on its plaster cast.

STEPPING BACK IN TIME

The hardened ash kept Pompeii safe for hundreds of years. But once uncovered, the city had little protection. Weather was hard on the ruins. Buildings and walls crumbled. Frescoes grew dull.

damaged fountain

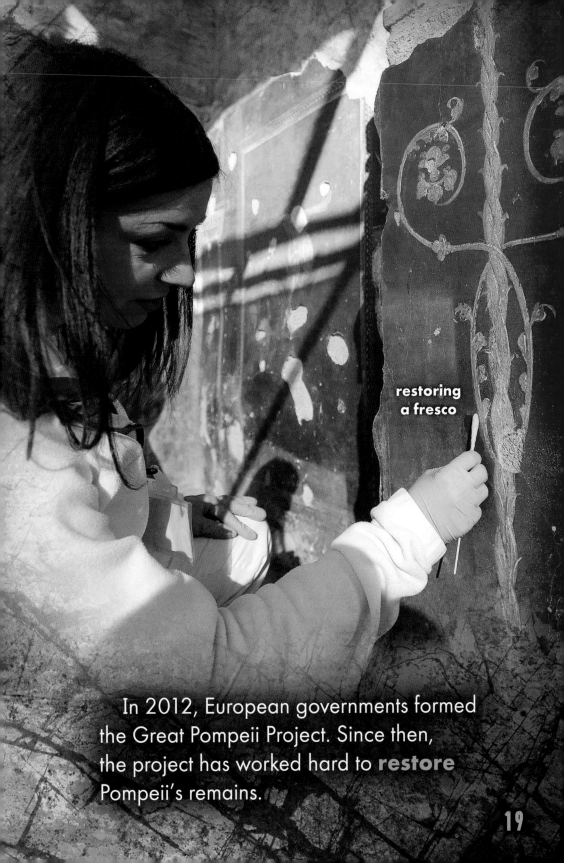

restoring
a fresco

In 2012, European governments formed
the Great Pompeii Project. Since then,
the project has worked hard to **restore**
Pompeii's remains.

19

DENTAL DISCOVERY

Discovery: Bones and teeth led to new
information about the people of Pompeii

Date of Discovery: 2015

Process:

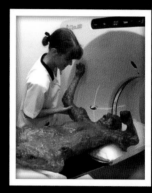

1. Took CAT scans of about 30 plaster casts from Pompeii
2. Studied victims' teeth and bones in the images
3. Found that remains were strong and healthy with a few exceptions

What It Means:

- Pompeiians ate healthy diets of fruit and vegetables
- Fluorine in the water led to healthier teeth free of cavities
- Damaged bones showed that some victims died from falling rocks

Visitors can travel through Pompeii and into its homes. They see Pompeii much like the Romans did before the eruption.

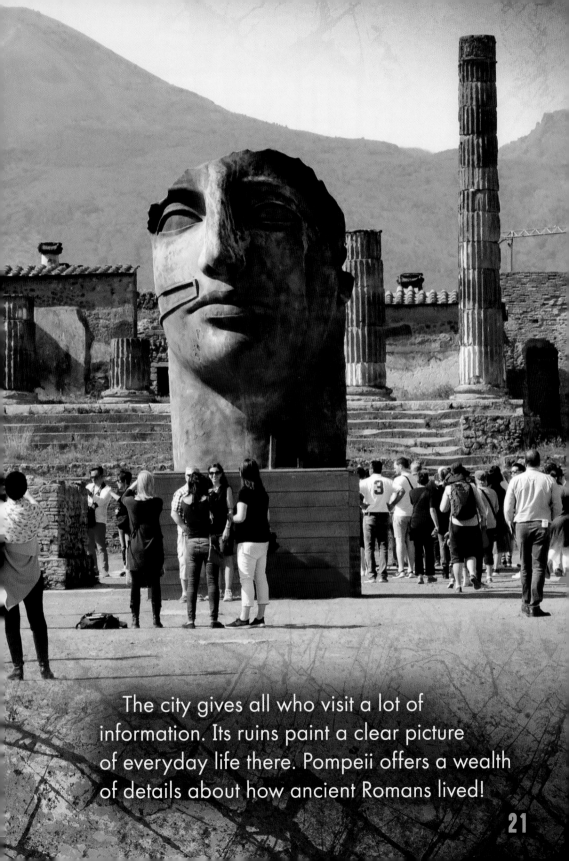

The city gives all who visit a lot of information. Its ruins paint a clear picture of everyday life there. Pompeii offers a wealth of details about how ancient Romans lived!

GLOSSARY

ancient—very old

casts—objects made to preserve the shapes of subjects

eruption—an event in which a volcano shoots out ash and gas

excavation—the act of digging up

forum—a central area in Roman cities where social, political, and religious activities took place

fresco—a wall painting

intense—strong or powerful

mosaics—decorations that use pieces of colored glass or tile to make pictures

perished—died

plaster—a pasty material that hardens when it dries

preserved—protected

restore—to rebuild an object to look as it once did

Roman Empire—a society under one rule that covered a large region, including parts of Britain, southern Europe, northern Africa, and western Asia; the Roman Empire lasted from 27 BCE to 467 CE.

ruins—the remains of human-made structures

temples—places of worship

victims—people who were killed or harmed

volcano—a hole in the earth; when a volcano erupts, hot, melted rock called lava shoots out.

TO LEARN MORE

AT THE LIBRARY

Conklin, Wendy. *You Are There! Pompeii 79*. Huntington Beach, Calif.: Teacher Created Materials, 2017.

O'Shei, Tim. *Secrets of Pompeii: Buried City of Ancient Rome*. North Mankato, Minn.: Capstone Press, 2015.

Waxman, Laura Hamilton. *Mysteries of Pompeii*. Minneapolis, Minn.: Lerner Publications, 2018.

ON THE WEB

FACTSURFER

Factsurfer.com gives you a safe, fun way to find more information.

1. Go to www.factsurfer.com.

2. Enter "Pompeii" into the search box and click 🔍.

3. Select your book cover to see a list of related web sites.

INDEX

ash, 11, 13, 17, 18

buildings, 8, 14, 15, 16, 18

casts, 17

discovery, 20

earthquake, 8

eruption, 11, 20

excavation, 12, 13

Fontana, Domenico, 12

forum, 14

frescoes, 16, 18, 19

graffiti, 13

Great Pompeii Project, 19

Herculaneum, 11

houses, 5, 15, 20

Italy, 6, 7

mosaics, 16

Mount Vesuvius, 5, 6, 8, 9, 11, 12

plaster, 17

Pliny the Younger, 9

restore, 19

Roman Empire, 6

Romans, 20, 21

ruins, 4, 15, 18, 21

Sarno River, 7

Stabiae, 11

temples, 5, 14

thermopolia, 14

timeline, 10-11

victims, 11, 17

volcano, 6, 9, 11

weather, 18